creative camera control

3rd edition

creative camera control

3rd edition

Peter Laytin

illustrations by Michael Ferreira

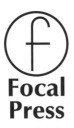

Focal Press

Boston Oxford Auckland Johannesburg Melbourne New Delhi

Focal Press is an imprint of Butterworth–Heinemann.

 A member of the Reed Elsevier group

Cover and text design: Lynn Sternbergh

Cover Photo: © 1998 Peter Laytin, *Cove at Torrey Pines*, San Diego, CA
Photos pages 88, 89: © Coelynn McIninch; all other photos: © Peter Laytin

∞ Recognizing the importance of preserving what has been written, Butterworth–
Heinemann prints its books on acid-free paper whenever possible.

 Butterworth–Heinemann supports the efforts of American Forests
and the Global ReLeaf program in its campaign for the betterment
of trees, forests, and our environment.

Library of Congress Cataloging-in-Publication Data
Laytin, Peter.
    Creative camera control / Peter Laytin ; illustrations by Michael Ferreira.—3rd ed.
        p. cm.
    Includes index.
    ISBN 0-240-80426-0 (pbk. : alk. paper)
        1. Photography—Amateurs' manuals. 2. 35mm cameras. I. Title.

    TR146 .L35   2000
    771.3--dc21

                                                                                00-049520

British Library Cataloguing-in-Publication Data
A catalogue record for this book is available from the British Library.

The publisher offers special discounts on bulk orders of this book.
For information, please contact:
Manager of Special Sales
Butterworth–Heinemann
225 Wildwood Avenue
Woburn, MA 01801-2041
Tel: 781-904-2500
Fax: 781-904-2620

For information on all Focal Press publications available, contact our
World Wide Web home page at: http://www.focalpress.com

10 9 8 7 6 5 4 3 2 1

Printed in the United States of America

This book is dedicated to my

students, past and present, and

to the memory of my parents,

Sylvia and Bernard, who offered

me choices and opportunities

from which to grow.

Acknowledgements

I would like to recognize and thank the following individuals and organizations:

Lynn Sternbergh and Alexander Laytin, who know all too well what this project entailed, Lynn Sternbergh for her patience, creative vision, and tireless effort in designing this third edition from cover to cover. Nancy Witting, whose friendship and dedication to this project enabled the structure and concepts to become clear. Adrianne Saltz, Josep Riera, George Peet, and Gabrielle Keller for their generosity and emotional support during the revisions for this edition. Adrianne Saltz for her editing of the revised writing. Jim Stone, Jim Haberman, Charles Meyer, Jim Sternbergh, Hunts Camera and Video, Lisa Boenitz, Marie Lee, Lilly Roberts, Coelynn McIninch, Rebecca Kiely, and Jenn Tuomala for professional and technical assistance. Mary Jane Ryan and the Boston Red Sox, Janet L. Heywood and Mount Auburn Cemetery, for access and assistance. MS, JR, BG, DP, PD, for support and suggestions.

Minor White, who shared his knowledge, quests, generosity, and friendship, and George Gambsky, who first lit the candle.

Finally, I would like to extend my deep gratitude to Michael Ferreira for his dedication and thoughtful, clear, and creative illustrations, which complement the text. I deeply appreciate his commitment to this project.

Contents

Charts, Diagrams, and Photographs

CHARTS

DIAGRAMS

PHOTOGRAPHS

Introduction

Creative Camera Control, 3rd Edition, is for beginning and intermediate photographers, and for
those who have recently acquired a camera.
Showing the inexperienced photographer how
to gain control, make creative decisions from
a foundation of knowledge, and increase self-
confidence is the motivating force behind this
book. In an easy-to-follow narrative, this step-
by-step approach to photography will lead the
photographer those few critical steps from
understanding the inter-relationship of all
aspects of the camera, lens, and film, to a level
of growing confidence that allows for creative
decision-making.

For new camera owners who are frustrated
by their camera manuals, for beginner photographers with no knowledge of camera work, for self-
taught photographers, and for those enrolled in
photography classes, the explanations, diagrams,
illustrations, and charts will be informative and
useful in acquiring camera control.

I believe that through *"conscious"* photography, the creative vision can easily be cultivated.
It is far more rewarding to know the potential of
the camera, lenses, and film, to understand how
they relate to each other, and to master control of
them than it is to occasionally make a great
photo due to luck or chance.

Through knowledge and conscious decision-making, an amateur photographer can acquire confidence and creative control over the camera. An understanding of two concepts will allow for unlimited creative possibilities and satisfaction: First, that all aspects of photographic control are related to each other (halves and doubles, explained throughout the book). Second, that one can learn to see and think the way a light meter "sees" the scene. What you will learn in this book will not necessarily allow you to use the camera more quickly, nor magically intuit proper exposures. However, you will learn the possibilities and limitations of each photograph. You will know *why* each photograph turns out the way it does, and *what* to do to accomplish a different result.

As cameras become more automated, offering many features and functions, the potential for becoming overwhelmed increases. The result is often the use of only a few features, which might not always achieve the desired result. There are choices, even with automated cameras, that will determine the success of a photograph.

The structure of this book is as close as possible to the teaching method I have successfully used for more than 25 years in introductory photography courses and workshops.

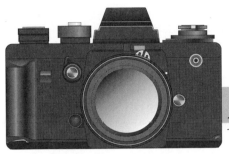

1: The 35 mm Camera

*The camera as we know it is derived from the **camera obscura,** literally "dark room." This 15th century device was used as an aid for artists' drawings until the 19th century. In 1837, when it was announced that "nature" could be recorded with a camera, the invention of photography was official.*

From the bulky and cumbersome early view-cameras to the extremely sophisticated 35 mm roll-film cameras of today, photography and the camera have continued to evolve. First introduced in 1925, the 35 mm camera is now the most popular size roll-film camera today, used by amateur and professional photographers alike.

Any camera is basically a light-tight box with a lens, which is often in a focusing mechanism. The lens has an aperture that controls the amount of light entering the camera. Light-sensitive film is held in place at the rear of the camera, opposite the lens, and is secured to a film advance mechanism. A shutter controls the duration of the light exposure, and a viewfinder allows for both composition and (in more sophisticated cameras) focusing.

Cameras are often grouped according to their format (the format is the negative size pro- *format* duced by the camera). Cameras are also classified by their design or optical viewing systems. Simple cameras (those with one set focus or those with two or three pre-set distances to choose from) are simply called "viewfinder cameras." Sophisticated 35 mm cameras (those that allow for variable focus) are called either single-lens reflex (SLR) or rangefinder cameras.

single-lens reflex (SLR) or rangefinder

SINGLE-LENS REFLEX (SLR) AND RANGEFINDER CAMERA

The simplest way to identify a single-lens reflex camera is to look for a bulge on the top center of the camera, which houses the viewfinder. The viewing system of a single-lens reflex camera is composed of a reflex mirror housed in the camera body, and a prism and focusing screen housed in the viewfinder. The rangefinder, which is flat across the top, uses a combination viewfinder (for composing) and simple prism (for focusing), located above and usually to the side of the lens.

DIAGRAM 1

SLR / RANGEFINDER CAMERAS

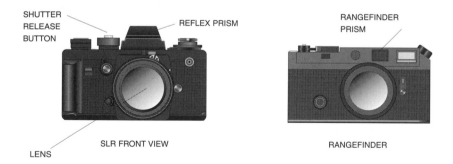

SHUTTER RELEASE BUTTON

REFLEX PRISM

RANGEFINDER PRISM

LENS

SLR FRONT VIEW

RANGEFINDER

Single-lens reflex and rangefinder cameras each have advantages and disadvantages. One is not inherently better than the other. Many people believe that the single-lens reflex (SLR) camera is superior because it allows you to look directly through the lens, while the rangefinder forces you to look at the prospective picture through a window off to the side of the lens. While it is true that the rangefinder camera is often at the low end of a manufacturer's camera line, some of the finest engineered and most optically advanced cameras are rangefinders.

SINGLE-LENS REFLEX		RANGEFINDER	
ADVANTAGES	**DISADVANTAGES**	**ADVANTAGES**	**DISADVANTAGES**
Through-the-lens composition (accurate composition)	Increased internal vibration	Less internal vibration (hence, inherently sharper)	Viewfinder composition (less accurate composition)
Effects of various lenses visible	Loss of visual contact during exposure	Constant visual contact	Effect of lens changes not visible
Accurate close-up copy-stand photography	Louder shutter	Quieter shutter	Parallax error in close-up/copy-stand photography
Numerous lens choices	Dim viewing system	Bright viewing system	No interchangeable lenses (some models)
	More moving parts	Fewer moving parts	
	Flash at sync speed or slower	Flash sync at any shutter speed (if leaf shutter)	

CHART 1

SLR AND RANGEFINDER CAMERA COMPARISONS

Advantages and Disadvantages

Inside the single-lens reflex camera, a mirror is positioned at approximately a 45° angle to the lens. This mirror reflects the light coming through the lens, directing it to a focusing screen and prism system at the top of the camera, where the image is reproduced right side up. In order to expose the film that is located directly behind the mirror (and shutter), the mirror must flip up, out of the way. After exposure, the mirror flips back down to its original position. This moving mirror creates a residual internal vibration at the moment of exposure, which may slightly diminish the sharpness of an image (when compared to a rangefinder).

When looking through the eyepiece of a rangefinder camera, you are looking through a window above and usually to the side of the lens. There is no internal "moving" mirror system for viewing. Therefore, there is no internal vibration

mirror

at the moment of exposure. A photograph from a rangefinder is inherently sharper than one from an SLR if all other variables are equal (i.e., engineering, optics, etc.).

When using different focal length lenses with the SLR, you can see the changes those different lenses create. This is because you are looking through the lens of the camera. Whatever you see through that lens is what will be recorded on the film. So, "what you see is what you get" with an SLR.

DIAGRAM 2

SLR / MIRROR PRISM

The rangefinder does not allow the same degree of composition control. Some high-quality rangefinder cameras allow you to change lenses, but the system for viewing and composing an image remains unchanged. When looking through the eyepiece you are still using the viewing system built into the camera body. Different focal-length lenses create different magnifications and spatial distortions, but you cannot see those changes. Therefore, you cannot compose accurately for them. You are changing the "taking" lens, the lens that records the picture, but you are not changing the lens in the viewfinder!

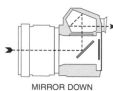

MIRROR DOWN

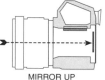

MIRROR UP

A good rangefinder camera with interchangeable lenses has a mechanism inside the viewfinder to guide you in composing, such as LED brackets that change position according to the lens. This mechanism gives a general parameter within which to compose, but again, it does not allow you to see distortion or changes in spatial relationships.

parallax error

With rangefinder cameras, the viewing system can create another type of composition problem: "parallax error" in close-up and copy-stand photography. What your eye sees in the viewfinder will be different from what the lens will record when focused on a subject less than 5 or 6 feet from the camera. An object that is centered in the viewfinder is actually recorded off-center on the film. The closer an object is to the lens, the more severe the problem. The only way to correct for parallax with a rangefinder camera is to guess how much to move the camera to properly center the subject for the "taking" lens. A rangefinder camera is therefore not the best choice for doing close-up or copy-stand work, situations where composition placement is critical.

There is no parallax error with an SLR. Again, what you see in the viewing system is what you get on the film.

SLR systems offer a great variety of lens choices, both from the camera manufacturer and from after-market lens manufacturers. Rangefinder cameras that allow interchangeable lenses are usually restricted to just the manufacturer's lens system.

With an SLR, the mirror is up for the fraction of a second when an image is recorded, blacking-out the viewing system. With a rangefinder camera one is able to maintain constant visual contact, even during the exposure. Some photographers say they prefer the range-finder to the SLR because of the loss of eye contact at the exact moment of exposure. However, for these few individuals, such reasoning may be philosophical rather than practical.

The SLR is a noisier camera. With the mirror flipping up and down, in addition to the snapping sound of its focal plane shutter (discussed later), the SLR is quite loud. The rangefinder camera, on the other hand, with no mirror to move, is relatively quiet. A photographer who needs to work inconspicuously in a crowd is far more obvious with an SLR. After just one shot — **CLICK** — everyone is aware of the photographer's presence. Some photographers and photojournalists prefer a rangefinder camera because it makes them less noticeable. It's a matter of choice and working style.

Another advantage of the rangefinder camera is that it usually has a brighter viewfinder than the SLR camera. This is especially advantageous in low-light situations.

An SLR has more moving parts than a

rangefinder camera. Its moving mirror system must be perfectly timed to the opening of its shutter. With the SLR, therefore, there is greater potential for camera problems and repairs.

sync speed

In flash photography, the SLR has a specific "sync speed." The camera cannot be used at a shutter speed faster than the "sync speed." However a rangefinder camera with a leaf-shutter can use any shutter speed for flash photography. (See pg. 77.)

Clearly, there are a number of considerations involved in choosing a 35 mm camera system. One system is not "better" than the other, except in terms of your own personal preferences and working style.

DIAGRAM 3

CAMERA BOTTOM

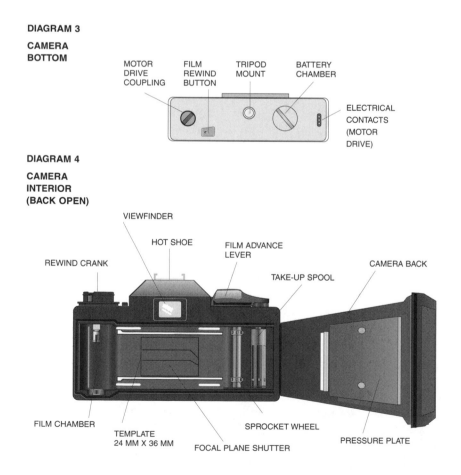

MOTOR DRIVE COUPLING   FILM REWIND BUTTON   TRIPOD MOUNT   BATTERY CHAMBER

ELECTRICAL CONTACTS (MOTOR DRIVE)

DIAGRAM 4

CAMERA INTERIOR (BACK OPEN)

VIEWFINDER

HOT SHOE

FILM ADVANCE LEVER

REWIND CRANK

CAMERA BACK

TAKE-UP SPOOL

FILM CHAMBER

TEMPLATE 24 MM X 36 MM

SPROCKET WHEEL

FOCAL PLANE SHUTTER

PRESSURE PLATE

LOADING AND REWINDING FILM

The film for 35 mm cameras comes in a metal, light-tight cartridge called a "cassette." The film feeds from the cassette through a felt light trap. Although the film measures 35 mm wide, the actual size of each negative is 24 mm x 36 mm. The half-width of film at the beginning of a roll is called the "leader" of the film.

cassette

In some cameras, raising the rewind crank post opens the camera back and allows the film to be placed in the film chamber. If you have to raise this post to get the film into the film chamber, then you need to lower it again to secure the cassette. Automatic winding and auto-load cameras may not have this type of post. In these cameras, the cassette slides in from the open bottom end of the film chamber up onto the post.

rewind crank
camera back
film chamber

Inside, usually attached to the camera back, is the pressure plate. The pressure plate holds the film absolutely flat against the rectangular window called the 35 mm template, which creates the format size (24 mm x 36 mm) parallel to the lens plane. If the film were allowed to buckle even slightly, the photograph would be out of focus.

pressure plate

template

Manual Load Cameras

After placing the cassette in the film chamber, stretch the leader across the template, then across the sprocket wheel and onto the take-up spool. When you advance the film, the sprocket wheel pulls fresh film forward and the take-up spool winds the film. Advance the film with the film advance lever once or twice, until you get past the film leader. Make sure the sprocket wheel is engaging the sprocket holes on the film. Close the camera back.

sprocket wheel

take-up spool

sprocket holes

Auto-Load Cameras

Secure the film in the film chamber. Stretch the leader across the template, then across the sprocket wheel and up to the designated mark in your camera body. Close the camera back. The film will automatically advance to the appropriate position.

Checking Proper Film Loading

When the film is properly loaded in a manual camera, the film rewind crank should move counter-clockwise every time the film is advanced.

Manual Load Cameras. After loading film and closing the back of the camera, advance the film once. This will re-engage the sprocket wheel. Now, gently *rewind* the film, *without* using the rewind release button (see pg. 12). This will take up any film slack in the cassette. As soon as you feel resistance (from the tightened film against the engaged sprocket wheel), STOP rewinding. With every film advance you should now see the film rewind crank move, as fresh film is pulled from the cassette. If the rewind crank is not moving, the film is not being pulled through the camera. Open the back to check whether the film has slipped off the take-up spool. Try loading it again.

Auto-Load/Rewind Cameras. Most motorized auto-load/wind/rewind cameras have a window to give you a visual clue for proper film loading. Check your specific manual.

Setting the Film Speed

exposure meter

Most cameras have a built-in exposure meter (see pg. 31) that calculates the intensity of the light and determines an appropriate exposure for the type of film you are using. (See "Film.") All film is standardized by a film sensitivity number designated by the International

ISO

Organization of Standards (ISO). (See page 56.) In older cameras, you must set the camera's meter to the sensitivity of the film you are shooting. There is usually a small dial containing the ISO settings.

Recent advances in manufacturing have made cameras able to sense the film cassette's

DX bar code, a combination checkered and bar code (see Diagram 5). When the DX code is electronically read by the camera's sensors, the ISO (ASA) film speed is automatically set for the meter system. Depending on the camera, the DX sensor might also enable the camera to signal the last shot, or automatically rewind the film after the last frame. Sophisticated DX sensors know whether the film being used is color or black and white, and allow for more difficult exposures with black and white film (black and white film has more latitude and is more forgiving than color film).

If you *manually* set the ISO (ASA) it must be re-set every time you change to a different speed film. Forgetting to reset the ISO is one of the most common mishaps in photography.

DIAGRAM 5
FILM CASSETTE

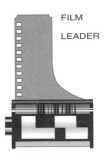

FILM LEADER

DX BAR CODE

Rewinding

At the end of shooting a roll of film, you *must* rewind the film back into the light proof cassette. Remember, the film is unprotected when it is outside the light proof cassette on the take-up spool.

You must rewind the film back into the cassette with the manual rewind crank (on auto-wind cameras, with the auto-rewind switch). Some auto-wind cameras rewind automatically after the last frame is exposed.

manual rewind crank
auto-rewind switch

Before you begin rewinding film on a manual camera, you must depress or activate the rewind

---

If you accidentally open a camera back without rewinding the film, light will expose and ruin the film. If this happens in a bright light environment, the film will have light leaks coming in from all edges, and will not be worth processing. (No matter how fast you close the camera back, you probably won't react faster than the speed of light!) But, if this accident occurs in a low-light situation, you react quickly in closing the camera back, and you are at the end of the roll of film, you might save the first few shots on the roll. This is because they may have been protected by the multiple revolutions of film around them. If the film is important to you, it might be worth it to go ahead with processing.

rewind release button

release button (sprocket wheel release switch), which releases the sprocket wheel gear from the forward direction. Trying to rewind without releasing the sprocket wheel would tear film between the sprocket holes by ripping it across the geared, stationary sprocket wheel. These tiny chips of film could then cause serious problems to the shutter mechanism.

On most cameras the rewind or release button is located directly below the sprocket wheel, on the bottom of the camera body. On some cameras it may be a lever located on the top or front of the camera body. The rewind post should remain down and engaged inside the cassette. The rewind crank usually has an arrow showing the rewind direction.

Motorized cameras have a switch for automatic rewind, which releases the sprocket wheel before rewinding. Some cameras automatically dump the film onto the take-up spool when the film is initially loaded and the camera back closed. Then, with each exposure, the film is automatically rewound back into the cassette.

With manual cameras, it is best to rewind the film slowly to avoid static build-up. This is especially true when you're in a cold or dry environment. Since the film is rewinding across a metal pressure plate and through the felt strips of the cassette, static charge can build up. The faster you rewind the film, the more likely this is to occur. Too much static build-up can create a discharge that looks like single or multiple streaks of lightning across the film. These streaks can occur anywhere on the film — across frame lines, between sprockets, and on the image areas. In extreme cases, static discharge can ruin an entire roll. Of course, if you have automatic rewind, you will not be able to control the rewind speed. Therefore, try to "ground" the camera, or your body, before rewinding. Touching the camera or a bare hand to an object that is grounded, like a piece of metal, or even touching snow-covered ground, will help prevent static discharge. If the camera is very cold, wait until you are indoors and the camera is at room temperature before rewinding the film.

THE CAMERA BODY

On most automatically controlled 35 mm cameras, adjustable rings and dials that control various functions have been replaced by control keys and mode buttons. A data panel (LCD) on the top surface of the body, or in the viewfinder, informs the photographer of the automatically selected or manually controlled aperture, shutter speed, and other information. Many SLR cameras have a depth-of-field preview button or manual switch. This switch allows you to look through the lens aperture (f-stop) that will be used at the moment of exposure. When you look through an SLR camera's viewfinder, you look through the largest possible f-stop opening for that lens, no matter what f-stop is set. At the moment of exposure it closes to the selected f-stop; after exposure it returns to the largest f-stop. You will not experience seeing the selected f-stop unless you preview it.

mode button

data panel

depth-of-field preview button or manual switch

The shutter release button is depressed to take or "receive" the photograph. A cable release can usually be screwed into the shutter release button for use in conjunction with a tripod. A cable release triggers the shutter release internally, without any physical movement or pressure on the camera. On the bottom of the camera, a female screw thread called a tripod mount can usually be found for attaching the camera to a tripod. A tripod is a three-legged support for a camera that can stand on the ground, the floor, or a table top. It is used when you want the sharpest shot possible or when you need to keep your hands free for other things. At very slow shutter speeds, it is difficult to hold a camera steady.

shutter release button

cable release

tripod mount

tripod

Another feature on many cameras is the shoe, located on top of the camera. The flash unit attaches to the camera by sliding onto this shoe. Most shoes are called hot shoes because they have small contact points that connect the electrical circuitry of the camera to the flash. This contact allows the flash to fire when the shutter

shoe

hot shoe

release button is depressed. There may also be other contact points on the shoe that allow "dedicated" flash. (See pg. 78.) Many cameras come with a flash built into the camera body; these have no shoe.

If the flash unit is too large to fit on the hot shoe, or if you want the light to come from a direction other than the camera position (for possibly an aesthetically more appealing light), then a special *sync cord* (PC cord) must be attached from the flash unit to a separate synchronization *sync terminal* (sync) terminal on the camera body, or to an adapter that attaches to the hot shoe. Electric current must trigger the flash when the camera's shutter release button is depressed.

self-timer   Some cameras have a self-timer that automatically releases the shutter internally, after a set time delay. The self-timer is often used when the photographer wishes to get into the photograph. It is also used to avoid hand holding a camera when a slow shutter speed is used and a tripod or cable release are unavailable. The camera can be placed on a ledge, table-top, or any available level surface, and the self-timer will release the shutter without excessive camera movement.

film-advance lever   Manual wind cameras have a film-advance lever for advancing film to the next frame, but *auto-wind* most cameras today are motorized (auto-wind), which eliminates the need for a film advance lever. The film advance lever or auto-wind mechanism accomplishes three things. First, it moves the take-up spool and sprocket wheel, pulling fresh film forward. Second, it changes the number in the film counter window. Third, and most importantly, it cocks or resets the shutter. (Older manual cameras allow for supplementary motor drives, which provide rapid film advance and shutter cocking for multiple frames-per-second shooting.)

THE SHUTTER

shutter   The shutter controls the amount of light that strikes the film by opening for a specific length of time. It can be controlled electronically, mechanically, or (with some cameras) both electronically and mechanically.

Focal Plane Shutter

There are two types of shutter systems: the focal plane shutter and the leaf, iris, or between-the-lens shutter. The focal plane shutter is the more prevalent shutter type. It is built into the camera body, near the film plane, beneath the template. The focal plane shutter can be made out of cloth, metal foil, and plastics, and can move horizontally or vertically. The film is exposed when a slit moves across the film. Focal plane shutters move in one direction only and can move at exceptionally fast speeds.

focal plane, leaf, iris, between-the-lens shutters

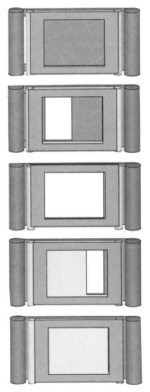

If you have a manual wind camera, open the back and take a look inside. When you advance the film and cock the shutter, you will see two sets of overlapping screens move either vertically or horizontally from a resting position to the opposite side of the rectangular template opening. When the screens move from one side of the window (at rest) to the other side of the window (cocked), the shutter is ready to be released. When you depress the shutter release button, the two screens will separate: the first screen releases and moves back to rest, creating a gap where light can strike the film, and the second screen follows, closing off the opening. You control how quickly the second screen follows the first by setting the shutter speed controls. To see the difference in shutter speeds, look through the back of the camera with the back open. Set the shutter speed to 1 second and release the shutter, then change to ½ second and release the shutter, and so on, continuing up the scale.

DIAGRAM 6

FOCAL PLANE SHUTTER

DIAGRAM 7
IRIS SHUTTER

IRIS, CLOSED

IRIS, PARTIALLY OPEN

IRIS, OPEN

IRIS, PARTIALLY
CLOSED

IRIS, CLOSED

Leaf, Iris, or Between-the-Lens Shutter

The leaf, iris, or between-the-lens shutter is built into the lens. It is made of thin metal leaves that open like the iris of an eye, from the center outward, and allows light to strike the entire film surface during the process of opening and closing down. Leaf shutters cannot be engineered to move as fast as focal plane shutters, since they have to open fully and then reverse to close back down. It's usually less expensive cameras, such as disk cameras, that have this type of shutter built into them, but some expensive camera systems also use the leaf shutter. If you open up the back of a camera and see the rear of the lens, you know it has a leaf shutter.

You can control the shutter speed for creative effect, using the shutter speed dial or the shutter mode switch, depending on your camera. The shutter speed is one of the important variables you should become knowledgeable about, to have full control over your photography.

Shutter Speed Stops

The standard shutter speed settings are actually reciprocals.

Some cameras are able to go to $\frac{1}{8000}$, but I would say $\frac{1}{8000}$ of a second is for photographing humming birds hiccuping. The majority of cameras go only to $\frac{1}{1000}$. "B" stands for bulb, meaning the shutter will stay open for as long as you have your finger on the shutter release button. "B" is used for long exposures, called time exposures (exposures longer than one second).

The shutter speed controls the length of the exposure. Each shutter speed stop halves or doubles the amount of light as the one next to it. For example, $\frac{1}{500}$ is half as much light as $\frac{1}{250}$, and $\frac{1}{4}$ is twice as much light as $\frac{1}{8}$. The only adjacent stops not perfectly halving or doubling each other are $\frac{1}{8}$ to $\frac{1}{15}$, and $\frac{1}{60}$ to $\frac{1}{125}$.

Manual and semi-automatic cameras must be set exactly on a shutter speed stop. Electronically controlled shutters found on most contemporary 35 mm cameras allow shutter speed stops to be set between full stops (e.g. at ¹⁄₄₅), but on manual cameras, speeds can't be set between ¹⁄₃₀ and ¹⁄₆₀ with the hope of producing a ¹⁄₄₅!

Every camera should show the shutter speed selected. If you can't move a dial or push a button to choose a shutter speed on your camera, you might be able to move the f-stop ring, thereby creating a corresponding change on the shutter speed scale. This scale would be located inside the viewing system or on top of the camera body. (See the section on the Aperture-priority (AP) system, pg. 33.) If your camera does not provide information as to the choice of shutter speed or f-stop to be used, the amount of creative control you have with your camera is limited.

CHART 2

SHUTTER SPEED STOPS

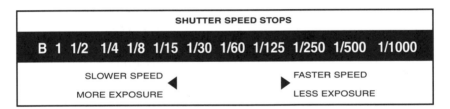

SHUTTER SPEED STOPS
B 1 1/2 1/4 1/8 1/15 1/30 1/60 1/125 1/250 1/500 1/1000

SLOWER SPEED ◀
MORE EXPOSURE

▶ FASTER SPEED
LESS EXPOSURE

Early shutters were triggered by air pressure in a sealed pneumatic cylinder. As the photographer squeezed a rubber bulb, the pressure opened the shutter. As long as the bulb was depressed the shutter remained open. Hence, the term "bulb" or "B."

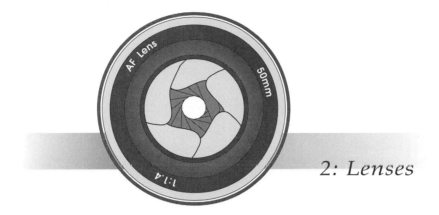

2: Lenses

A lens is a piece of glass or other transparent material made with surfaces that force rays of light to diverge or converge to make an image. A photographic lens is made up of a number of separate lenses, each of which is called a lens element. The lens elements are mounted within a cylinder of plastic or metal called the lens barrel. This barrel has an adjustable focusing ring on it. When an autofocus (AF) lens is mounted on an autofocus camera, a motor in the lens or camera body will adjust the focusing ring gears. The lens might also have an f-stop ring on it that adjusts the aperture inside the lens barrel. A lens is designated by its focal length. Examples of different focal length lenses include 28 mm, 35 mm, 50 mm, 150 mm, 250 mm, 35 – 70 mm, and 70 – 210 mm.

lens element

lens barrel
focusing ring
autofocus (AF)

f-stop ring

focal length

THE FOCAL LENGTH

Different focal length lenses create different effects in your photographs. Basically, the focal length controls *image size or magnification* and *angle of view.*

The focal length of a lens is the distance from the optical center (rear nodal point) of the lens to the plane of sharp focus for light rays from infinity.

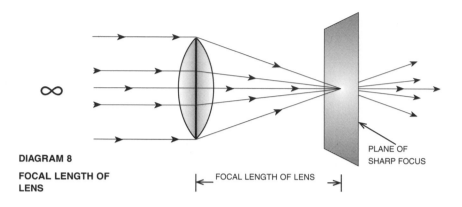

DIAGRAM 8

FOCAL LENGTH OF LENS

FOCAL LENGTH OF LENS

PLANE OF SHARP FOCUS

AUTOFOCUS LENSES

focus-lock

The technology of autofocus lenses is constantly improving, with advancements in the speed of focus, sensitivity in low light and selectivity. The newer lenses generally allow for quick and accurate focusing, but there can be problems. To overcome some of the problems with autofocus systems there is a focus-lock switch. This allows you to focus on a subject of main interest, lock that distance on the lens, and then reframe the composition, moving the main subject off-center. When purchasing an autofocus lens, make sure it has a manual override of the autofocus. It should allow for "smooth" focusing and ease of use, and it should give accurate results. Some autofocus systems focus the lens at the point where the photographer's eye is looking when the shutter button is pressed. Autofocus camera systems now make up the majority of new 35 mm camera sales.

LENS TYPES

In 35 mm photography, lenses with a focal length of 50 mm (40 mm–55 mm) are called normal lenses. Focal lengths greater than 50 mm are called "long lenses," and less than 50 mm, "short lenses." The commonly accepted term for a long lens is telephoto lens. The commonly accepted term for a short lens is wide angle lens. There are also "zoom" lenses, which have a variable range of focal lengths. Zoom lenses are the most popular lens in the amateur market today.

normal, telephoto, wide angle, and "zoom" lenses

Normal Lens

The normal lens for a 35 mm camera is a 50 mm lens. A range of focal lengths, from 45 mm to 55 mm, is also considered normal, but the 50 mm is the most common. Since the eye does not see the way a 50 mm lens sees, why should it be considered a "normal" lens? The human eye sees a peripheral range of about 180°. A normal lens has approximately a 47° angle of view. The normal lens definitely edits out much of what the naked eye sees. The "normal" human eye, when staring at a specific point, keeps that one point sharp; the remaining field of vision increasingly blurs towards the periphery. When a lens focuses on a specific point, let's say 10 feet away, everything on that plane 10 feet away is in focus, from top to bottom, left to right. What is "normal" though, are the objects' sizes and space relationships to each other as they recede in the distance. When I look down a tree-lined country road, there is a certain distance between me and the first tree, the first tree and the second tree behind it, between the second and third tree, and so on. As the trees recede, they appear smaller and smaller. When looking through a 50 mm lens, the trees will have the same spatial and size relationships to each other as they would to my naked eye. With a normal lens, objects appear as they would to the naked eye, in terms of size and proportion.

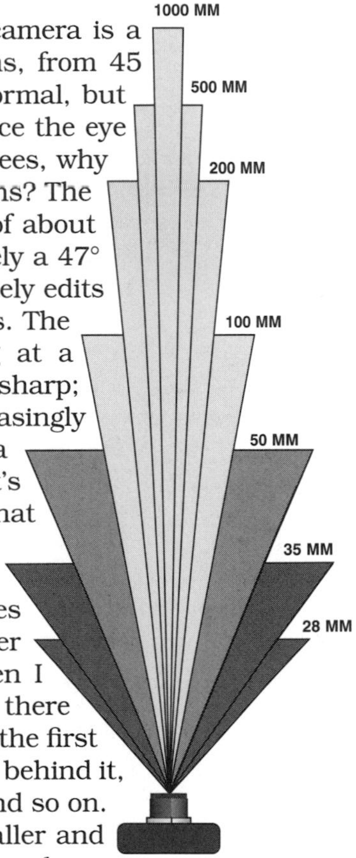

1000 MM
500 MM
200 MM
100 MM
50 MM
35 MM
28 MM

DIAGRAM 9

LENS FOCAL LENGTH AND ANGLE OF VIEW

Wide Angle Lens

A lens with anything less than a 50 mm focal length is called "wide angle." The standard wide angle lenses are 35 mm, 28 mm, 24 mm, and 20 mm. Next, depending on the manufacturer, come

19 mm, 18 mm, 17 mm, and 16 mm, followed by highly specialized and unique wide angle lenses called "fish-eyes." If you own a 50 mm lens, a 28 mm wide angle lens would be a good choice for a wide angle lens. A 35 mm lens is not different enough from the everyday 50 mm "normal" lens to be a popular choice for a first wide angle lens purchase. Many photographers actually use a 35 mm lens as their everyday normal shooting lens. Below 35 mm, lenses begin to create dramatic shifts.

Wide angle lenses have a greater angle of view than a normal lens. As you go to an increasingly wide angle lens, your field of view increases, and the scene itself appears to shift farther away from the camera. The wider the angle of the lens, the farther away and the smaller objects will appear. In order to maintain the same size subject with a wide angle as with a normal lens, you need to place the camera closer to the subject.

The major effect of a wide angle lens is the apparent distortion in spatial relationships. An object close to the camera will become abnormally large in size and proportion compared with objects farther away. The wider the angle lens, the greater that apparent distortion becomes.

Telephoto Lens

Telephoto lenses magnify objects and make them appear much closer than they really are. This is because telephoto lenses compress space, bringing objects closer together visually. As the focal length increases, the angle of view (angle of acceptance) decreases, and the distance between objects receding in space is more compressed.

Standard telephoto lenses in 35 mm photography are 85 mm, 105 mm, 135 mm, 200 mm, 300 mm, 500 mm, and 1000 mm. There are disadvantages to extremely long lenses. The longer the lens, the heavier it is, and therefore the more difficult to hold steady. Not only are objects magnified; very slight camera movements are also magnified. A slight movement that might not affect the image from shorter focal length lenses

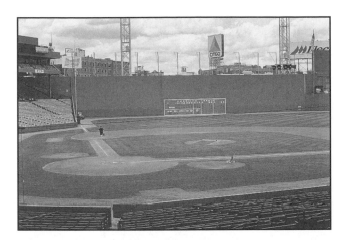

**ANGLE OF VIEW
(SUBJECT
VIEWED FROM
THE SAME DIS-
TANCE)**

50 mm
Normal lens

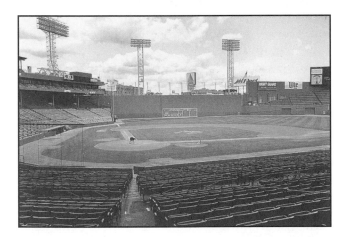

28 mm
Wide angle lens

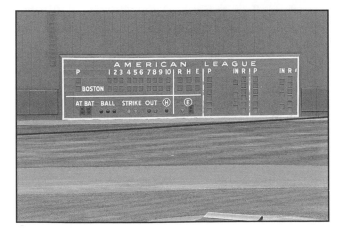

200 mm
Telephoto lens

can create a blurred image from a long telephoto lens.

Zoom Lens

Zoom lenses have a varying range of focal lengths. When photographing with a zoom lens, you don't have to be concerned about which focal length is used. While looking through the camera, you move the lens barrel zoom ring (which changes the focal length) in or out until the magnification or angle of acceptance is aesthetically pleasing. The advantage of a zoom lens is in its ease and convenience. It has the ability to provide the focal lengths of many fixed lenses all within one lens. But there are drawbacks. Zoom lenses are often heavier in weight and provide a slower "speed" lens (see pg. 29) than fixed lenses.

In the zoom lens is a set of moving elements. These moving elements cannot be perfectly positioned for all focal lengths; therefore, a zoom lens might not be as sharp as a fixed focal length lens of the same quality. Inexpensive zooms are not worth your time or money. Your photographs will never be crisp and sharp. If you want to buy a zoom lens, take the money that you would have spent on two fixed focal length lenses and put it towards the best zoom lens you can afford. Look at the zoom purchase as a way to avoid changing lenses in the field, not as a means of saving money. There are many excellent lens manufacturers, and with new computer formula lenses the quality is extraordinary. Good zoom lenses are tack-sharp and worth the investment.

Portrait Lens

Many photographers enjoy using a short telephoto lens for portraiture, usually one between 70 mm and 105 mm. Such a lens permits the photographer to be at a slightly greater distance from the subject than with a normal lens. This greater space is more comfortable for many photographers and their subjects, allowing for a more relaxed portrait. Also, the slight telephoto focal length, at close focus, will minimize distortion of facial features in portraits, over the normal lens.

Macro Lens

Macro lenses allow you to photograph within inches of your subject. They allow extreme close-up work, with an object to negative size ratio up to 1 to 1. The lens optics correct for aberrations caused by close focusing distances. Macro lenses have been built into all the categories of lenses, but the most popular macro lenses are the 50 mm and 100 mm lenses, and macro zoom lenses.

Teleconverter

A teleconverter is an inexpensive attachment that fits between the lens and the body of the camera and effectively increases the focal length. The most common teleconverters are 2x and 3x (extenders). A 2x converter will double the focal length; a 3x will triple it. Unfortunately these attachments reduce the amount of light two or three stops (respectively) and introduce aberrations that affect the clarity and sharpness of the lens. A better choice is to save the money and put it towards a telephoto lens.

LENSES AND PERSPECTIVE

There is a popular misconception that the focal length of a lens controls perspective. However, perspective is controlled only by the distance the lens is from the subject. If a telephoto lens and wide angle lens were used from the same distance from a subject, the perspective would remain the same; only the field of view would vary. The subject would seem farther away in the wide angle shot and closer in the telephoto shot. But if a section of the wide angle shot were blown up to match the telephoto image, the photographs would be exactly the same.

If a telephoto lens and a wide angle lens were used to take a shot of an object, that object would be the same size in the foreground of both

▼

Perspective is controlled only by the distance the lens is from the subject.

photographs only if the wide angle lens were moved much closer to the subject than the telephoto lens. This change of distance would create a dramatic change in perspective between the foreground object and its background. The telephoto lens would compress the space, while the wide angle lens would exaggerate the foreground-to-background distance.

F-STOPS

aperture
diaphragm

An aperture is the area, or size, of the lens opening regulated by an iris diaphragm. An aperture opening is designated as a mathematical ratio called an f-number. The ratio between the focal length of a lens and the diameter of the aperture opening is a specific f-number or f-stop. It is nothing more than a simple equation: the focal length of a lens divided by the diameter of the aperture.

f-stop

$$\frac{\text{focal length}}{\text{diameter of aperture opening}} = \text{f-stop}$$

$$\frac{(100 \text{ mm})}{(25 \text{ mm})} = f/4$$

Example:
If a 100 mm focal length lens has a 25 mm diameter aperture opening, then it would be calibrated as an f/4.

▼
*The f-stop
is the focal
length of a lens
divided
by the
diameter of
the aperture.*

A 50 mm lens with a 12.5 mm diameter aperture would also be marked f/4. If that same 50 mm lens had its diameter adjusted to a 25 mm opening, it would then be f/2. The larger the opening, the smaller the f-number.

$$\frac{(50 \text{ mm})}{(12.5 \text{ mm})} = f/4$$

$$\frac{(50 \text{ mm})}{(25 \text{ mm})} = f/2$$

At the same f-stop, all lenses admit the same amount of light. If the same f-stop is set on two different focal length lenses, the aperture diameters will differ, but the same ratio will be maintained (see the two f/4 examples on pg. 26). An f/8 on a telephoto lens allows the same image brightness as an f/8 on a wide angle lens, and so it is with any f-stop.

Although these numbers seem haphazard, with no progressive relationship to each other, each is actually the previous number multiplied by the square root of 2.

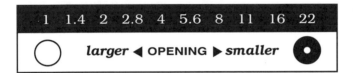

CHART 3

STANDARD
F-STOPS

Like shutter speed settings, each f-stop setting halves or doubles the amount of light as the next f-stop setting. *This is important to understand.* F/8 lets in twice as much light as f/11, and f/2.8 is half as much light as f/2. Halfway between one f-stop to halfway between the next f-stop is also one full stop, or halving and doubling (see Chart 4). Unlike shutter speeds, f-stops can be set anywhere between the full stop markings,

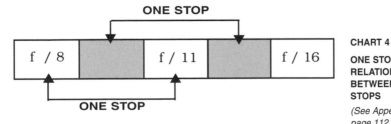

CHART 4

ONE STOP
RELATIONSHIP
BETWEEN HALF
STOPS

(See Appendix 3, page 112.)

whether or not there are physical click stops. Computerized cameras show the in-between stops on the screen readout.

DIAGRAM 10

**F-STOP
RELATIONSHIP**

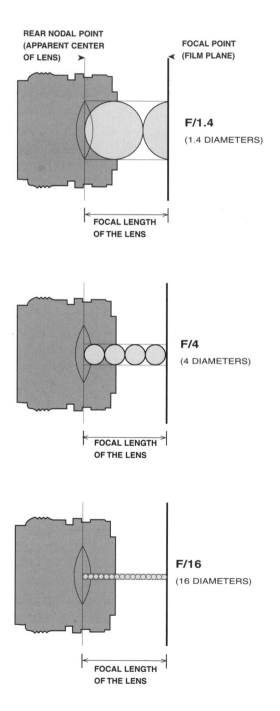

REAR NODAL POINT
(APPARENT CENTER
OF LENS)

FOCAL POINT
(FILM PLANE)

F/1.4
(1.4 DIAMETERS)

FOCAL LENGTH
OF THE LENS

F/4
(4 DIAMETERS)

FOCAL LENGTH
OF THE LENS

F/16
(16 DIAMETERS)

FOCAL LENGTH
OF THE LENS

Speed of a Lens

The largest possible f-stop opening of a lens is called the "speed" of a lens, or "maximum effective aperture." An f/1.4 is a "faster" lens than an f/2, because it admits more light and therefore permits a faster shutter speed (hence "speed of a lens"). A "fast" lens costs more than a "slow" lens, if all other factors are equal (i.e., same focal length, manufacturer, etc.). Unless you plan to do a lot of low light photography without using a flash or other additional light sources, buying a "fast" lens is usually not worth the additional investment.

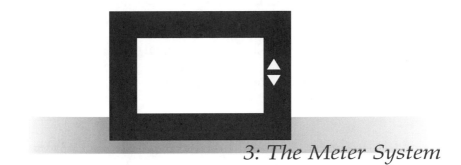

3: The Meter System

When loading film, it is imperative to set the proper film speed on the camera to correctly cue the internal light meter. An automatic camera with DX sensor will take care of this automatically. If you are using a separate, hand-held light meter, the meter will have to be set to the speed of the film in your camera. The light meter, whether built into the camera or hand held, will determine the correct exposure by analyzing the existing light in relationship to the film sensitivity. The meter will then set or determine the f-stop and shutter speed combination to be used.

REFLECTED VERSUS INCIDENT METERING

The built-in camera meter is a reflected-light meter, one that reads the light reflecting off or emitted from the objects in the field. This reflected or emitted light is called "luminance." The reflected-light metering system allows metering from the camera position. With hand-held meters there is usually a choice of reflected-light or incident-light metering. With incident metering, a diffusion dome is placed in front of the sensor, the meter is placed at the subject, and the sensor is pointed back towards the camera position. This method measures the light falling upon, not reflecting off, the subject. The intensity of incident light is called "illuminance."

reflected light

luminance

incident light

illuminance

TYPES OF METER SENSING

The photocell in the meter system is either a selenium cell (Se), cadmium sulfide (CdS), silicon (Si) photodiode (SPD), or gallium arsenide phosphide (GaAsP) photodiode (GPD). Manufacturers approach the possibilities of sensor placement differently, but all allow for the meter system to be one of four basic types: averaging, center-weighted, spot, or matrix.

Averaging meters are sensitive to the entire range covered by the lens.

Center-weighted meters give more attention to the center area of the viewfinder, but still incorporate readings from the edges.

Spot meters give total attention to the center area. Some systems allow you to use an exposure memory lock to lock in a spot reading. Some allow the possibility of averaging a few different "spot" readings, if so desired.

Matrix meters read light from myriad sensors and analyze the information through a microprocessor. These meters try to distinguish the subject from the background. A few matrix meters allow you to pre-program the microprocessor to weight the readings towards, say, greater depth-of-field (for landscapes), or faster shutter speed (for action photography).

Some cameras incorporate two or three of the above methods in their metering system.

METER DISPLAYS

In most cameras, the viewfinder displays the data gathered and information about exposure. The symbol, needle, dots, or numbers can be displayed by a physically moving mechanical pointer, *LED* LED (Light Emitting Diode) lights, or LCD (Liquid *LCD* Crystal Display) digital displays.

The built-in meter system is integrated with the controls of the camera system; that is, it is directly coupled to the f-stop and shutter speed of the camera. Camera systems have different methods for letting the photographer know what exposure is needed. Your camera meter might use a match-needle arrangement (the f-stop ring controlling one, while the shutter speed ring controls the other). When the needle and what it has to match bisect, you have proper exposure.

**DIAGRAM 11
METER DISPLAYS**

You might have a meter system that requires you to line up a needle between a (+) and (-) sign, or a system where you see in the viewfinder a panel with a range of shutter speeds or f-stops. In this situation, when you adjust the f-stop or shutter speed control the meter changes a light or needle inside the viewfinder, designating a choice from the panel.

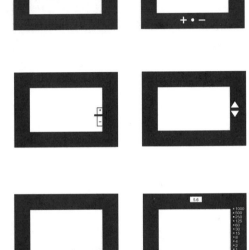

Manual Setting

A manual camera requires the physical setting of both the f-stop and shutter speed scales.

Automatic Setting

A sophisticated automatic camera has any one of the following Automatic (A) adjustments, or modes: Aperture-priority (AP), Shutter-speed priority (SP), and Program (P). Your automatic camera might allow one, two, or all three of these possibilities, as well as a manual (M) override of the automatic selection.

With an "Aperture-priority" (AP) camera, you select the f-stop and the camera automatically selects and sets the shutter speed. Conversely,

aperture-priority

Shutter-speed priority   with a "Shutter-speed priority" (SP) camera, you choose a shutter speed and the camera automatically determines and sets the appropriate f-stop. There is no need to align anything. Many computerized cameras allow you to choose between these two priority systems. If the camera has a *Program* "Program" (P) mode, the camera automatically chooses both an f-stop and shutter speed combination in response to the intensity of the light striking the meter. You relinquish any choice in the creative decision-making process to the engineer who designed the camera. At least if you choose an f-stop or shutter speed, you're making a decision that will affect the photograph. In "Program" mode you have no creative input!

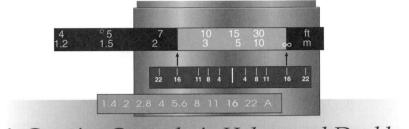

4: Creative Control via Halves and Doubles

Creative control becomes much simpler when you begin to understand that all camera manipulations and choices are related to each other in terms of halves and doubles. This concept applies equally to f-stops, shutter speeds, and film ISO.

THE STOP

The "stop" is a measure of change in exposure based on the amount of light reaching the film. It is referred to when f-stops and shutter speeds are changed, as well as when describing the difference in film speeds (see ISO, pg. 56). A one stop increase in exposure doubles the amount of light reaching the film. This increase can be achieved by setting the next larger aperture opening or by doubling the exposure time. A one stop decrease in exposure lets half the amount of light reach the film, either by setting the next smaller aperture opening or halving the exposure time.

▼
This concept of "halves and doubles," along with understanding the light meter (discussed in Chapter 6) form the basic foundation for creative camera control.

Controlling Exposure: Shutter Speeds and F-Stops

Two controls determine film exposure: the shutter speed and the f-stop. These controls work together to regulate the amount of light that strikes the film. The f-stop controls the amount of light allowed through the aperture, and the shutter speed controls the length of time the light is

▼
An exposure is an f-stop and shutter speed combination.

allowed to strike the film. In other words, an exposure is an f-stop and shutter speed combination.

RECIPROCITY LAW

$T \times I = E$

The Reciprocity Law states that Time (T) x Intensity (I) = Exposure (E). If the time is doubled and the intensity is halved (or the time is halved and the intensity doubled), the exposure (the result) remains the same.

Equivalent Exposures

equivalent combinations

When your camera indicates an exposure combination, it is but one of many equivalent combinations, any of which would give proper exposure!

Example:
Your camera shows that a combination of f/5.6 at ⅟₆₀ would give a proper exposure. However, any equivalent combination would also give the proper exposure. If you changed the f-stop to f/8, the camera would have chosen ⅟₃₀ as the proper accompanying shutter speed. (See chart below.)

CHART 5

EQUIVALENT EXPOSURES

EQUIVALENT EXPOSURES								
f/22	f/16	f/11	f/8	f/5.6	f/4	f/2.8	f/2.0	f/1.4
4	8	15	30	60	125	250	500	1000

One stop less light (or half as much light on the f-stop scale) combined with one stop more light (or twice as much light on the shutter speed scale) gives you an equivalent amount of light striking the film.

Example:
Your camera designates f/11 at ⅟₃₀ as the proper exposure. You decide you want a faster shutter speed, and set the camera to ⅟₂₅₀. The meter system adjusts and indicates that f/4 is required for an equivalent and proper exposure.

$$\frac{f/11}{30} = \frac{f/4}{250}$$

+ 3 stops increase (more light)

- 3 stops decrease (less light)

0 exposure change

A small f-stop opening for a long period of time is the same amount of light as a large f-stop opening for a short period of time. (For information about Reciprocity Failure, see *Miscellaneous Tips* on page 95.)

Many novice photographers use the first f-stop/shutter speed combination their camera suggests. The resulting picture is properly exposed, but may not have the "look" the photographer intended. In many cases an equivalent f-stop and shutter speed combination could have accomplished the desired effect, because each combination produces a slightly different look. At times there are numerous possible combinations to choose from. Only *you* know what you are trying to accomplish in a photograph, so it is up to you to choose the proper equivalent. Don't leave it up to your camera to decide. A carefully chosen exposure combination can mean the difference between a creative photograph and a memory notation!

CREATIVE CONTROL: THE EXPOSURE COMBINATION

Example:
*You took your last shot with the camera set at f/11. For the lighting conditions of your next shot, the camera's metering system shows you that the shutter speed should be ⅟₆₀ **for an f/11** f-stop. You now have a proper exposure combination, but you may want to choose an equivalent combination for a different visual effect.*

What if the photograph is dealing with motion or fast action? Would a faster shutter speed be desirable?

An aesthetic decision must be made to decide which f-stop/shutter speed combination best suits the situation and your intention.

Remember, there is almost never only one choice or possibility. Take the time to consider other possibilities. You need to be conscious of

CHART 6

EQUIVALENT EXPOSURE COMBINATIONS

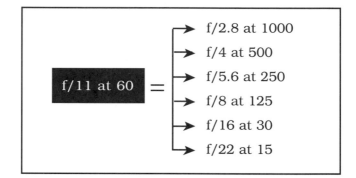

f/11 at 60 =
- f/2.8 at 1000
- f/4 at 500
- f/5.6 at 250
- f/8 at 125
- f/16 at 30
- f/22 at 15

what you are doing. If you want to **control** the medium and **be creative** with the camera, you must **slow down**, **think**, and **choose** your exposure combinations carefully. ***Consciously choosing the exposure combination that best suits the situation is the path towards creative camera control.*** Remember, each equivalent f-stop and shutter speed combination will give a properly exposed photograph, but each will look different. It is possible that only one combination will produce the photograph that best fulfills your intention.

▼

There is almost never only one choice or possibility.

Simply put, you must ***choose one variable to control***. If the variable you choose is the shutter speed, then you have to accept the corresponding f-stop for that specific lighting condition. Conversely, if you choose to set the f-stop, you must accept the shutter speed the meter system designates. Whenever you decide on one variable, you have no choice as to the other variable. If you don't like the corresponding variable shown by the meter system, alter your initial variable until the combination becomes acceptable. If you find no acceptable exposure combinations, don't take the picture.

The Shutter Speed Choice

If the subject matter is moving, or the photograph is about motion, you must make a decision in terms of the shutter speed. A moving subject is visually important and usually primary to the success of a photograph. Once you decide on a specific shutter speed, you are locked into a specific f-stop for proper exposure. Under specific light conditions, only one f-stop is going to link with a specific shutter speed.

▼
For creative camera control, you consciously set either the f-stop or the shutter speed, depending on your purpose.

3 Guidelines of Relative Motion. But how do you go about deciding what shutter speed to use? When choosing one shutter speed over another, there are three guidelines to keep in mind: speed, direction, and distance.

1. Speed. First, consider the speed of a moving object. How fast is the moving object going?

You will need a faster shutter speed to stop the action of a running jackal than you will need for a walking dog. A horse at full gallop might be "stopped" with an exposure of ⅟₅₀₀ or ⅟₁₀₀₀ of a second, while a tortoise at full gallop might take only a ¼ to ⅛ second exposure.

To "freeze" the action of fast moving subjects, a fast shutter speed is necessary. For slower moving subjects, a slower shutter speed is possible.

2. Direction. Second, consider the direction in which the object is moving.

A train going across your field of vision needs an extremely fast shutter speed to stop the action — let's say ⅟₁₀₀₀ shutter speed. If you stood on the track with the train coming directly at you, you might stop the action with only a ⅟₂₅₀ shutter speed.

An object moving toward or away from the camera needs a slower shutter speed to "freeze" the action than an object moving across the field of vision, which needs a faster shutter speed.

To understand this better, think about riding in a car. When you look straight ahead through the windshield, telephone poles, streetlights, or cars in the opposite lane seem to approach you more slowly than when you turn your head and look out the side window. In this orientation, the same telephone poles, streetlights, and cars appear to fly right by.

The direction the subject is moving in relationship to the camera is also an important factor.

3. Distance. The third factor to consider is the distance between you and the moving object.

For example, a 60 mph train is traveling across your field of vision, 20 feet away from you. You can stop the action with a very fast shutter speed. If the same train, moving at the same speed, were traveling in the same direction across your field of vision, but 1 mile away on a mountain pass, you could probably render it "stop-action" with a very slow shutter speed. At that distance, the train appears to creep along the mountain.

The farther a subject is from the camera, the slower the shutter speed necessary to "freeze" the action.

CHART 7

SHUTTER SPEED RATES

RATE	SLOW		MEDIUM		FAST
SHUTTER SPEED	1 2 4 8	15	30 60	125	250 500 1000

So how do you know which shutter speed to use? There is no easy answer. You learn through experience and trial and error. You'll find you extrapolate when an object is moving on a diagonal towards you, or when a certain object is moving slower than the last time you photographed it. Speed, direction, and distance must all be kept in mind to make an informed choice, an intelligent guess.

Should you always stop the action of a moving object? Not necessarily. The slight blur of an object in a photo might actually be desirable. It gives the impression of activity, indicates that movement was taking place, or implies motion. If a man jumping over a log were stopped with a fast shutter speed, the photograph might look strange, with the man's body frozen in space. Although the perfectly sharp person might look interesting, that isn't how the eye normally perceives such movement. You would be extracting that person from reality. If the same situation were photographed at a slightly slower shutter speed, thus creating a blurred figure, the photograph would talk about a person in motion jumping from one side of the log to the other. It would imply movement in a two-dimensional still image. Consider your intention before choosing a shutter speed.

Movement offers many creative possibilities. You might want to transform what you see using motion.

You could set your camera on a tripod and point the lens down at a stream with swiftly running water breaking around some rocks. Take one shot with a fast shutter speed, and you'll get stop action of running water with splash droplets suspended and floating in mid-air. From the same location, on the next frame, choose a very slow shutter speed. The result might resemble an aerial photograph of low lying clouds with mountain peaks breaking through the clouds. The rocks might become the tops of mountains and the blurred rushing water might be transformed into lush white clouds.

Panning is a technique whereby the moving object is relatively sharp and the background is blurred in the photograph. This is accomplished by moving the camera during the exposure, so the subject remains in the same position in the viewfinder. It is important to begin the pan before releasing the shutter and to continue the steady movement until well after the shutter has closed.

panning

DEPTH-OF-FIELD

VARYING F-STOP (CONSTANT LENS AND DISTANCE)

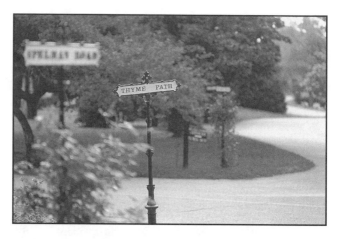

Subject taken using f/1.4

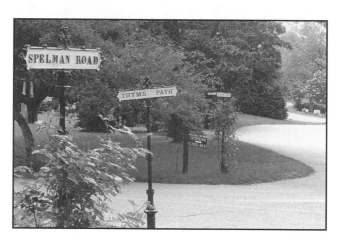

Same subject taken using f/22

Three Factors Controlling Depth-of-Field

1. F-stop

2. Focal length

3. Camera to subject distance

The 3 factors that control the depth-of-field are the f-stop, the focal length and the camera to subject distance.

You choose the f-stop when you want a particular depth-of-field. The depth-of-field is a variable zone of acceptably sharp focus in front of and behind the object the lens is focused on. The choice of f-stop determines how shallow or deep this zone of focus will be. After you select the f-stop, the meter system will determine the shutter speed necessary for proper exposure.

If you begin to think and conceive of your

photograph in the way that the camera lens records it, you will become aware of your ability to control the range of focus around your subject!

Many manual-focus lenses (particularly fixed focal length normal and wide angle lenses) have a depth-of-field scale. However, many auto-focus and

---

The smaller the f-stop opening, the greater the range of sharp focus. The larger the f-stop opening, the narrower or more shallow the range of sharp focus.

DIAGRAM 12

CIRCLES OF CONFUSION

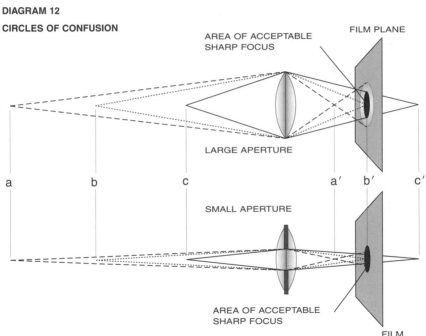

Subject at distances (a), (b), and (c) are focused at (a'), (b') the film plane, and (c'). Discs of light, called circles of confusion, are projected on the film plane from (a), (b), and (c). With the large aperture, (a') falls outside the area of "acceptable" sharp focus and will be considered out-of-focus; (b') is pin-point sharp; (c') falls within the area of acceptable sharp focus. The small aperture creates smaller discs that allow (a'), (b'), and (c') to fall within the area of acceptable sharp focus.

most zoom lenses do not have a usable or functional depth-of-field scale.

The depth-of-field scale is located on the lens barrel, usually between the f-stop scale and the focusing ring scale. This immovable scale has the focusing index mark located at its center. Symmetrically placed on either side of the focusing index mark are lines marked with numbers referring to f-stops. Manufacturers give varying attention to the readability of the depth-of-field scale. Some include all the possible f-stop numbers, and others just a few. Still others, like Nikon, use color-coded lines, printing the f-stop on the f-stop ring in the same color as the number on the depth-of-field scale. Some zoom lenses do have a depth-of-field scale, generally a set of converging curved lines.

When you focus a lens with a depth-of-field scale, the subject's distance is indicated just above the focusing index mark on the distance, foot/meter (ft/m) scale. When properly focused, the subject will be sharp as long as the camera does not move during the exposure. In addition, an area in front of and behind the subject will also be sharp. This depth-of-field is generally divided into a ⅓ to ⅔ ratio around the subject; that is, ⅓ of the range of sharp focus is

DIAGRAM 13

DEPTH-OF-FIELD SCALE (NORMAL LENS)

FOCUSING RING

DISTANCE SCALE (FEET/METERS)

DEPTH-OF-FIELD SCALE

F-STOP SCALE

DIAGRAM 14

DEPTH-OF-FIELD SCALE (ZOOM LENS)

FOCUSING RING

DISTANCE SCALE (FEET/METERS)

DEPTH-OF-FIELD SCALE

F-STOP SCALE

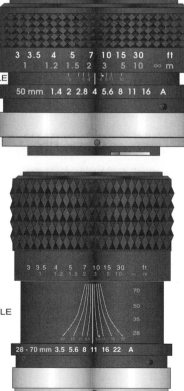

in front of the subject, and ⅔ of the range of sharp focus is behind the subject. The range of that space can be increased by choosing a small f-stop opening, or decreased with a large f-stop opening.

The closer the subject is to the camera, or the longer the telephoto lens, the more even the ratio becomes (½ in front to ½ behind).

The range of sharp focus is the distance shown between the two markings on the depth-of-field scale for the f-stop selected.

▼
For any given focal length, you control the range of sharp focus with the f-stop.

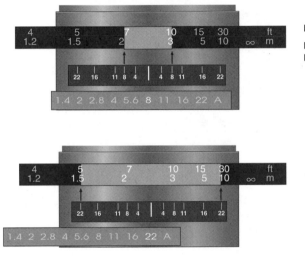

DIAGRAM 15

DEPTH-OF-FIELD: F/8 AND F/22

Note:
If you do not have a depth-of-field scale on your lens remember that the smaller the f-stop opening, the greater the depth-of-field and the more you will have in sharp focus. The larger the f-stop opening, the shallower the depth-of-field will be.

WAYS TO USE THE DEPTH-OF-FIELD SCALE

Probably half of all photographs taken by amateurs are taken with the lens focused at infinity. Generally the intention in these cases is to get as much in focus as possible.

**DEPTH-OF-FIELD
VARYING FOCAL
LENGTH**

**(CONSTANT:
F-STOP AND
DISTANCE)**

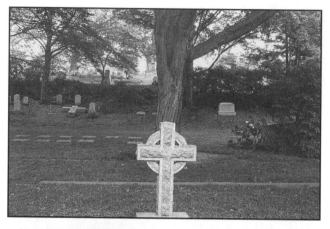

*subject taken with **28 mm lens***

▼

*The shorter the
focal length of a
lens, the greater
the depth-of-field
at any chosen
f-stop.*

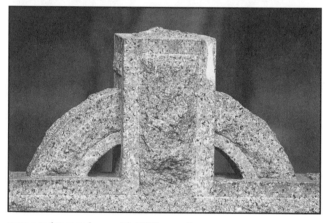

*same subject taken with **200 mm lens***

Hyperfocal Focusing

Hyperfocal focusing is an attempt to obtain
the maximum depth-of-field for any selected
f-stop. If the infinity (∞) symbol on the focusing
ring is set over the mark on the depth-of-field
scale that corresponds to the selected f-stop to
be used, then the photograph will have the
maximum depth-of-field for that f-stop. The
greatest distance in focus will always be infinity.
The nearest point of sharp focus will be approximately half the distance from that indicated
above the focusing index mark. The distance

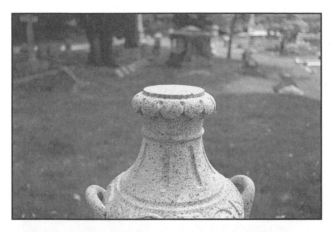

**DEPTH-OF-FIELD
VARYING
DISTANCE
(FOCAL POINT)**

**(CONSTANT:
LENS AND
F-STOP)**

*subject focused at **3 feet***

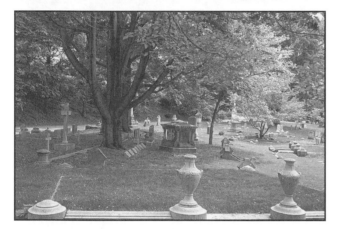

▼
*The depth-of-field
increases as
the camera-to-
subject distance
increases.*

*same subject focused at **16 feet***

directly above the focusing index mark is called
the "hyperfocal distance."

Example:
*Focused at ∞, the depth-of-field is 15 ft. – ∞
using f/16. The nearest point of focus, 15 ft., is the
"hyperfocal distance." Adjust the focus so the
hyperfocal distance is over the focusing index
mark. When the lens is set at the hyperfocal distance, the maximum depth-of-field is achieved. The
new depth-of-field is now 8 ft. – ∞, an increase in
the amount of foreground in focus.*

▼
*To find the
hyperfocal
distance, set the
∞ mark over the
focusing index
mark. The fore-
ground distance
shown over the
selected f-stop,
on the depth-of-
field scale, is
the hyperfocal
distance.*

DIAGRAM 16

HYPERFOCAL FOCUSING (AT F/16)

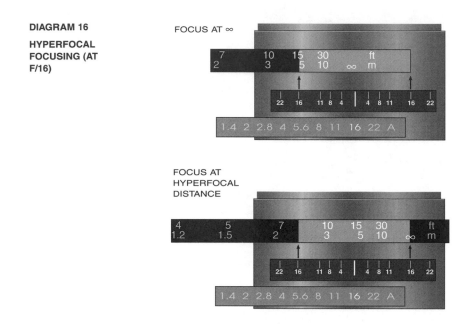

FOCUS AT ∞

FOCUS AT HYPERFOCAL DISTANCE

shallow depth-of-field focus

When you focus or look through a lens, you are always looking through the largest possible f-stop opening for that lens, no matter what f-stop is set. This shallow depth-of-field enables you to focus on your subject; you can read off the lens the subject's distance from the camera. The only area that looks sharp is located at the distance shown above the focusing index mark. At the moment of exposure, however, the lens closes down to the selected f-stop, thereby creating the proper depth-of-field for that f-stop (as indicated on the depth-of-field scale). This occurs simultaneously with the mirror flipping up (on SLRs) and the shutter opening. When the exposure is completed, the mirror flips back down and the lens returns to the shallow depth-of-field of its largest f-stop opening.

depth-of-field preview

If you want to preview the depth-of-field before the exposure is taken, you may do so if your camera has a depth-of-field preview switch or a manual "M" switch. In all honesty, it is a pretty useless control. To preview the depth-of-

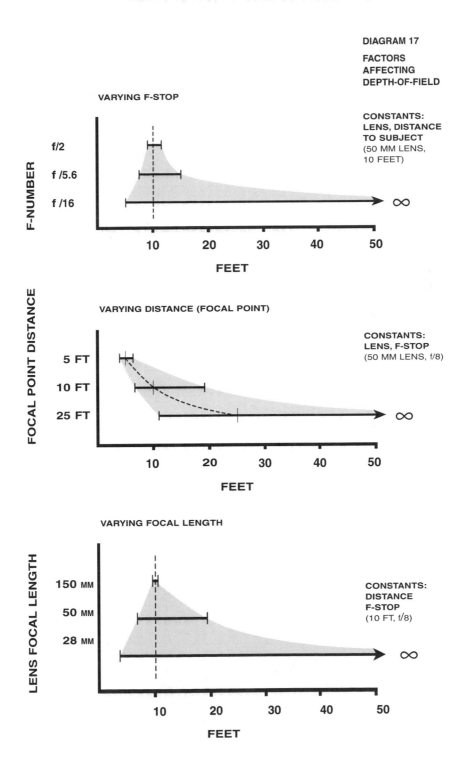

DIAGRAM 17

FACTORS
AFFECTING
DEPTH-OF-FIELD

VARYING F-STOP

CONSTANTS:
LENS, DISTANCE
TO SUBJECT
(50 MM LENS,
10 FEET)

F-NUMBER

f/2

f /5.6

f /16

∞

10   20   30   40   50

FEET

VARYING DISTANCE (FOCAL POINT)

CONSTANTS:
LENS, F-STOP
(50 MM LENS, f/8)

FOCAL POINT DISTANCE

5 FT

10 FT

25 FT

∞

10   20   30   40   50

FEET

VARYING FOCAL LENGTH

CONSTANTS:
DISTANCE
F-STOP
(10 FT, f/8)

LENS FOCAL LENGTH

150 MM

50 MM

28 MM

∞

10   20   30   40   50

FEET

field at a small f-stop opening, the lens aperture closes down and makes the viewfinder so dark that it is difficult to discern what is indeed sharp. If you have a depth-of-field scale, you can be far more accurate in predicting what your photograph will accomplish. You can refer to it to see what distances will be acceptably sharp in the photograph.

Zone Focusing — Advanced Depth-of-Field Control

Zone focusing is a method for predetermining a range of sharp focus for the photograph using the depth-of-field scale.

Example:
Walking along a country road, you come across a beautiful old apple tree in the middle of a field. You look at the scene and decide you want the focus to extend from the hand-built stone wall in the foreground to the white clapboard farm house way in the distance. (Obviously the apple tree will be sharp if the planes in front and behind it are.)

1) To zone focus, you focus first on the nearest object you want sharp, the stone wall, and look at the distance scale on the lens to determine that it is 8 feet away.

2) You focus next on the farthest object you want sharp, the farmhouse, and look again at the focusing mark to see that the distance is infinity (∞).

3) Moving the focusing ring, you place these two symbols so they lie equidistant from the focusing

DIAGRAM 18

ZONE FOCUSING
8 FEET — ∞

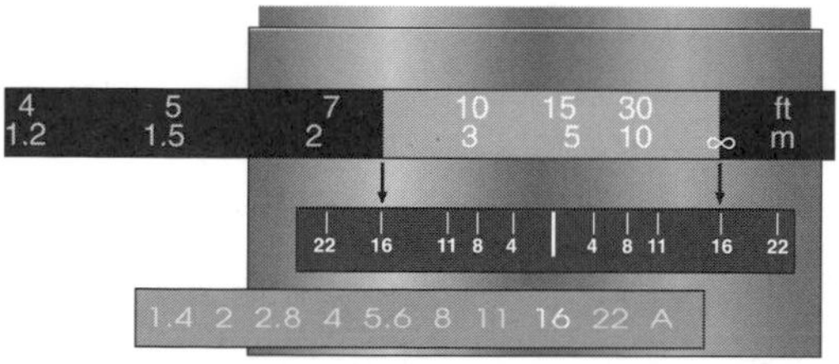

index mark. The focusing mark acts as the ful-
crum between these two distances. The symbols
8 and ∞ now line up over (or possibly in-between)
the same f-stop markings on either side of the
focusing index mark on the depth-of-field scale.

The marker shows that what is going to be
sharp is 15 feet away. But, what actually will be
in focus is the range that exists between the
f-stop markings on the depth-of-field scale for
that selected f-stop.

4) You leave the lens focused as is and *manually
set* the camera to the indicated f-stop, f/16. Next
you determine the shutter speed exposure that
corresponds to f/16 in this lighting condition.
You have now consciously decided the proper
exposure and range of focus you want for your
photograph.

Some autofocus cameras can accomplish
this zone focus via a specific "depth-of-field"
mode setting. After activating this mode, you
focus on the closest point you want in focus, then
the farthest point. The camera automatically
remembers these distances and sets the necessary f-stop needed. You then reframe the photograph in the viewfinder. The range of sharp focus
has been calibrated, the appropriate f-stop has
been set, and the needed shutter-speed has been
set. If the camera can't set the parameters you
select, it signals you.

Zone Focusing and Creative Freedom. Almost
all amateur photographs are taken with the subject "dead center" in the frame, exactly where the
focusing ring is located. More often than not this
creates a very static composition. Don't let the
focusing ring impose itself on your compositions.
Zone focusing can give you the freedom for more
creative compositions and a fresh vision. Even if
you choose not to zone focus, you can improve
your composition by reminding yourself to
reframe the scene after focusing. If you focus on
a centered object and then reframe it on the left
or right side of the frame it will still be in focus

and the resulting photograph may have a more dynamic composition. Remember, the camera is still the same distance from the subject. Even with an autofocus camera, you can lock the focus on the subject and then re-compose the picture.

Zone focusing is also extremely helpful when you want to shoot swiftly and spontaneously. For example, in "street" or candid photography, it is sometimes difficult to focus on a moving object such as an interesting looking person who is walking towards you. Often you do not have enough time to get them in focus before they pass by. In situations like that, why not set a zone of sharp focus?

Example:
Stand on the sidewalk and focus first on a parking meter 12 feet away and then on one 25 feet away. You want to set that space in sharp focus so that anyone walking through that space would be in focus. Set those two distances equidistant on the depth-of-field scale and determine the f-stop needed. Now, find out what shutter speed corresponds to that f-stop.

If the chosen f-stop gives you an acceptable shutter speed, leave the focusing ring alone. Now anyone who walks into that pre-determined range will be in focus. All you need to do is wait for the right person, situation, or event to occur in that space. You don't have to be concerned with focusing directly on any single moving object. You have now set the stage to give yourself creative freedom for seeing and shooting spontaneously.

If the shutter speed is too slow for your wishes, there are three choices. You can use a faster ISO film, decrease the depth-of-field (larger f-stop opening uses a faster shutter speed), or stand farther away (which will allow you to use a larger f-stop opening and maintain the same depth-of-field). Remember, the closer you are to the subject, the shallower the depth-of-field.

The central location of all focusing systems often results in "centered" and static composition. The optimum camera design for creative results would place the focusing ring at the bottom corner of the viewing screen. Focusing would then require the photographer to shift the camera upward. Once the focus was set, the photographer would re-compose. Camera designs being what they are, the zone focusing method is the next best guarantee that you will re-compose each picture in the viewfinder after focusing for the required depth-of-field.

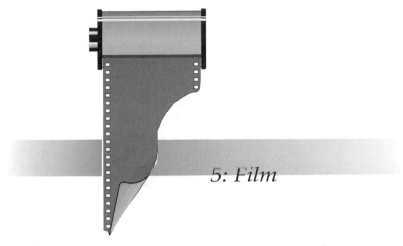

5: Film

Understanding both technical and conceptual aspects of film can help you obtain creative control.

FILM STRUCTURE

Basically, film is made by coating a light-sensitive suspension on a cellulose ester support base. The light-sensitive suspension, the emulsion, is made of silver halides and gelatin. Silver halide (silver salt) crystals are light sensitive. Color films are similar to black and white films except that they have dyes coupled with the layers of silver halides. In different emulsions, the silver halides vary in size and arrangement. Some manufacturers produce particularly unique films. Eastman Kodak's T-grain film is composed of flat-tabular crystals, whose multi-faceted surface picks up more light than conventional silver salts. Konica's "monodisperse crystals" and Agfa's "twin-grained" flat and compact crystals are examples of other unique technologies. Each attempts to optimize speed and grain characteristics.

The rear surface of film is coated with an antihalation dye that absorbs light. The dye coating prevents light from penetrating through the base, which would scatter or reflect off the pressure plate and back through the film.

ISO/ASA/DIN

A standard terminology called ISO (International Organization of Standards) numbers, or film speeds, categorizes the light sensitivity of all film emulsions. At one time there were two systems in use: the no-longer-used ASA (American Standards Association) numbers, arithmetically related to each other; and the German DIN (Deutsche Industrie Normen) logarithmic numbers represented with a degree (°) symbol. ISO is represented as ASA/DIN° (e.g., Tri-X film ISO 400/27°). ASA and DIN have been phased out, and the ISO system is now universally used for categorizing film sensitivity. The American Standards Association has now become ANSI, the American Standards Institute. One might also find terminology related to the non-standardized EI (Exposure Index) when discussing film.

It is universally accepted that the ASA and ISO numbers are interchangeable. The camera's metering system must be set to the light sensitivity of the film in the camera. This can be done either manually or (as previously discussed) automatically, through DX coding.

DIAGRAM 19

FILM

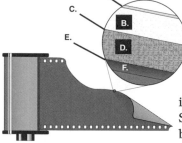

A.   ANTI ABRASION SUPERCOAT

B.   EMULSION

C., E.   SUBBING (ADHESIVE)

D.   FILM BASE

F.   ANTIHALATION BACKING

CHART 8

ISO/ASA/DIN EQUIVALENTS

(See Appendix 1, page 111 for a complete table.)

ISO	ASA	DIN
25/15°	25	15
32/16°	32	16
50/18°	50	18
64/19°	64	19
100/21°	100	21
125/22°	125	22
160/23°	160	23
200/24°	200	24
400/27°	400	27
1000/31°	1000	31
1600/33°	1600	33
3200/36°	3200	36

Each ISO/ASA film speed number is ⅓ stop faster than the preceding one.

(Note: Only the ASA part of the ISO number will be used when discussing film speed. The standard ISO/ASA numbers are shown here.)

6	8	10
12	16	20
25	32	40
50	64	80
100	125	160
200	250	320
400	500	650
900	1000	1250
1600	2000	2500
3200	4000	5000

CHART 9
ISO/ASA
FILM SPEEDS

HIGH VERSUS LOW ISO/ASA

As a rule, the higher the ISO number, the less light the film needs for a proper exposure. The trade-off is that it produces a "grainier" looking photograph. The larger you blow up the image, the more obvious the grain will be. For some, a grainy photograph is an aesthetic preference. The choice of film helps determine that final "look."

Beware: Some photographers fall into the trap of *always* choosing a fast film (high ISO number). But there are many everyday situations where a 400 ISO film is *too* sensitive. For

CHART 10

ISO CHARACTER-ISTICS

LARGER GRAIN	LESS LIGHT NEEDED	LOWER ACUTANCE	**HIGHER ISO NUMBER**
SMALLER GRAIN	MORE LIGHT NEEDED	HIGHER ACUTANCE	**LOWER ISO NUMBER**

example, you should think twice about taking 400 speed film to a sunny beach. Your camera's smallest f-stop and fastest shutter speed might not be able to close out enough light. In this case, the film is too sensitive, too fast. Shoot with less sensitive, "slower" (lower ISO) films in bright situations, or use a neutral density (ND) filter to reduce the light intensity (see pg. 87).

It's a good idea to have a range of different speed films on hand at all times. If you refrigerate your film, you can easily extend the expiration date. If you freeze the film, you can slow the aging process even further. Film that has been refrigerated or frozen must be brought to room temperature before opening the plastic cap on the film container, because rapid temperature changes can cause condensation on the film, ruining it. A minimum warm-up time of one hour for refrigerated film and four hours for frozen film is suggested.

FILM SPEEDS: HALVES AND DOUBLES

Remember, all of photography is based on halves and doubles. That goes for the ASA rating of film, too. A film that is rated 400 is twice as sensitive, or twice as fast, as a film rated 200, and therefore needs half as much light or one stop less light to be correctly exposed. Likewise, a film rated at 50 is half as sensitive, with half the speed of a film rated at 100, and needs twice as much light or one stop more light to be correctly exposed.

Example:
Two photographers with identical camera systems photograph the same scene at the same time side by side. Lynn has 100 speed film in her camera. Alex has 400 speed film in his camera. Both make proper exposures using an f-stop of f/11. The difference is in the f-stop/shutter speed combination for the two cameras. With a 100 speed film in her camera, Lynn determines that at f/11 the necessary shutter speed is ⅟₆₀. With 400 speed film, Alex determines the necessary shutter speed to be ⅟₂₅₀ at f/11.

This is a two-stop difference. From 100 ISO to 200 ISO is one stop, and from 200 to 400 is another stop. So Alex needs exactly two stops less light for proper exposure. The camera's metering system automatically gives the necessary combination, and Alex uses a faster shutter speed.

In the above example, if the shutter speed had been the constant, there would have been a two-stop difference in f-stops needed.

All other things being equal, you need more light striking the film with the lower ISO film speed. A low ISO film is "slower" film than a high, "faster" film. The difference between 50 ISO film and 400 ISO film is 3 stops of light, just as between 400 ISO film and 3200 ISO film.

PURPOSEFUL "OVER" AND "UNDER" EXPOSURE

DX Override

Almost all films are DX coded. Most cameras that automatically read this DX code allow the photographer to manually override the DX setting and create a purposeful over or under exposure of the film.

Exposure Compensation Dial

Most other cameras have an exposure compensation dial. This dial allows you to adjust the exposure from +2 stops overexposure to -2 stops underexposure in half-stop increments. On some cameras +1 is designated x2 (double the exposure, or one stop more light); +2 is designated as x4 (quadruple the exposure, or two stops more light), -1 as x½ (one-half the exposure, or one stop less light); and -2 is designated as x¼ (one-quarter the exposure, or two stops less light).

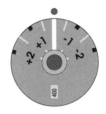

DIAGRAM 20

EXPOSURE COMPENSATION DIAL

FILM CHARACTERISTICS

Technically, films can be categorized according to the following characteristics: Color Saturation, Color Balance, Contrast, Grain, Sharpness, Resolution, and Latitude.

▶ **Color Saturation** is the density of a color.

▶ **Color Balance** is the relationship of exposed film to the original scene, or its accuracy, usually based on skin tones in midday sunlight.

▶ **Contrast** is the range of densities the film is able to record.

▶ **Grain** is the size, shape, and distance between

developed silver crystals. An important aesthetic factor in choosing a film; grain affects one's impression of sharpness and resolution as well as maximum enlargement size.

▶ *Sharpness* is the ability of the film to produce a distinct edge between two tones.

▶ *Resolution* is the ability of a film to reproduce fine detail.

▶ *Latitude* is the ability of the film to give acceptable results with over and under exposure. Black and white films have a greater latitude than color films, and negative producing films have a greater latitude than slide films.

Many film manufacturers, like Kodak, Ilford, Agfa, Konica, and Fuji, make excellent and highly regarded films. Film choice is a matter of personal preference.

FILM TIPS

Film and X-Rays

X-rays and airport security systems will affect your film. The higher the ISO rating of the film, the more susceptible it is to damage. X-rays are cumulative, just as they are in the human body. One or two doses might not affect the film, but a number of doses received through various airport screenings can destroy it. Security personnel will usually tell you that x-rays do not affect film. But have they ever asked how many flights and security checks you'll be going through on your trip? Always ask to have your film "hand checked." If necessary, lead lined film bags, available at photo shops, will effectively repel x-rays. But, beware! In high security countries, the officials may increase the x-ray intensity to the point where they penetrate the lead bag. At that intensity, the film would be instantly "fried" — ruined. Some airlines routinely x-ray "checked" baggage. So, film placed beneath the plane (in "checked" baggage) may no longer be safe.

Changing Film in the Middle of a Roll

With a manual rewind camera, you can

change film in the middle of a roll and reuse it later. A motorized camera also permits this if your auto-rewind allows a part of the film leader to protrude from the cassette after rewinding.

Before you remove the half-used roll, note your last frame number. Next, engage the rewind release button and start slowly rewinding. When you reach the beginning of the film, you will *hear and feel* the leader of the film disengage from the top sprocket of the sprocket wheel. As soon as you feel this release, *stop rewinding.* At that point, rewind just one-half turn more and open the back of the camera. The leader will be protruding from the cassette, ready for reloading at a later time.

When it is time to reload this roll of film, load it as usual and close the camera. Then place the lens cap on the lens and advance and shoot continuously up to the unused frame. Since no new light has struck the film, all the original exposures are unaffected. To play it safe, add two extra blank shots to avoid any overlap between the last shot (first loading) and the first shot (second loading). Note that on automatic cameras you must have the camera set to Manual to trigger the shutter with the lens cap on!

Labeling Film

It is a good idea to label film immediately after removing it from the camera. Indicate any personally useful information, such as location, date, or subject. With partially shot film, also include the last frame number. Some photographers carry a roll of masking tape in their camera bag for this purpose. I use removable "stick-on" (i.e., Post-It™) file folder labels. They take up less room and they leave no adhesive residue. These labels can also be attached to the camera body or case, and can help those of us who have trouble recalling what was on the first part of a roll of film in a camera not often used.

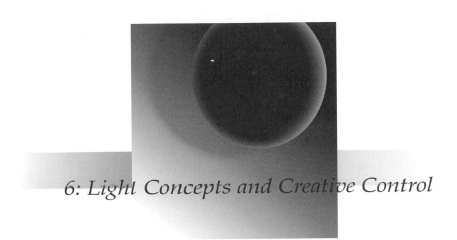

6: Light Concepts and Creative Control

A basic understanding of light concepts can help you match light to your subject and purpose, giving you greater creative control.

USING DIRECTIONAL LIGHT

As a photographer, it is important for you to be sensitive to the direction and quality of light falling upon the subject. If you carefully consider the effect that different directions of light might have on your subject, then you can match the lighting to your purpose and increase your chances of producing a successful photograph. In photography, there are four basic types of directional light: front light, side light, back light, and revealing light. In order to determine the type of light falling upon your subject, look at the subject's shadow. (Don't look at your own shadow, because you may be in a different type of light than your subject.) Look to the subject's shadow to determine the light. You will know that you are dealing with directional light when the shadow of the subject is equal to or greater than the subject itself. When the shadow is shorter than the subject, it is considered "top light," and the creative possibilities of using the directional light are diminished.

▼

Look to the subject's shadow to determine the light.

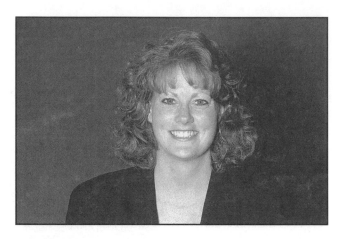

FRONT LIGHT

Front Light

Front light comes from behind the photographer's shoulder, falls directly upon the subject, and casts a shadow behind the subject. The effect of these shadows is not important since they are mostly blocked by the subject. Front or direct light lowers the contrast range of the scene, fills in the subject's surface shadows, and reduces the perception of texture and volume. With the sense of volume diminished, you have flat features. (Direct flash also produces this type of light. To avoid this quality of light, photographers often bounce-flash, or use a flash held off-camera.)

Example:
Imagine in your mind's eye a front-lit redwood forest. The light fills in the bark, eliminating the sense of texture and volume. Massive shadows from the trees are cast backwards into the forest. Just a few yards into the scene, the photographed forest would seem very dense and uninviting, because of the darkness.

Side Light

In side light, the subject's shadow is cast off to the side. One side of the subject is lit, while the other side is in shadow. With side light there is a strong sense of volume and texture. Side light is subconsciously a very powerful light. There is a

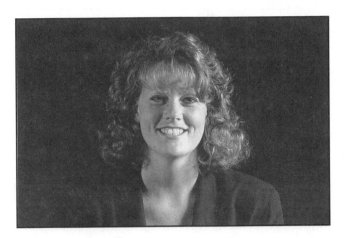

SIDE LIGHT

distinct vertical line that separates the light side from the dark side. There is a dichotomy between the light and dark. A tension exists in these tonal opposites, in this separation between light and dark. Metaphors such as positive/negative, black/white, yin/yang, and good/bad will play a part in the interpretation of the viewer. The vertical line that separates the light from the dark is itself important. Throughout all of art history, vertical lines have stood for strength and power, for reaching to the heavens. In contrast, horizontal lines have always stood for rest, calm, tranquility, and peace.

See for yourself. Bend your lower arm from the elbow and hold it vertically in front of you. Now bend it so it is horizontal. The vertical and horizontal positions of the arm connote very different qualities. Is an arm with a clenched fist more powerful looking when it is held vertically or horizontally?

Imagine again in your mind's eye that same redwood forest, this time side-lit. The tree shadows are cast off to the side. Half the trees' bark is lit, showing detail and volume, while the other half remains in shadow, a reinforcement of texture and form. The vertical line that separates the light side from the shadow side of the trees echoes the trees' verticality.

▼

You can manipulate the emotions of the viewer ever so subtly by controlling the way light strikes your subject.

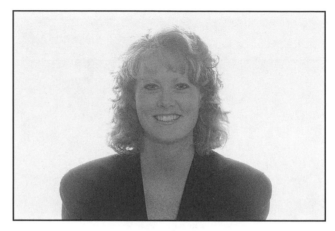

BACK LIGHT

Back Light

Back light comes from behind the subject, casting the shadow to the front. You have back light when the subject stands in front of a bright window, or with an open sky. Back light creates strong contrast between the light source and the shadow cast in the foreground. The foreground subject usually has very little detail. Back light is a very alluring light that draws you in. It has almost a religious connotation because of the "halo" effect it gives to some subjects. Hollywood actresses are often photographed in back light to create sensual appeal.

Imagine the redwood forest in back light, the source of light coming from deep within the forest. The shadows are now cast towards you. The edges of the trees are shimmering: the dark side of the bark shows little texture. The forest has almost a spiritual presence, and you might feel drawn to enter the scene. Without correction, the trees would be a pitch black silhouette, and not very inviting. But you can make a conscious creative decision to control it.

Revealing Light

Revealing light is the light that exists on an overcast day, or the light cast by fluorescent lights. It is a broad, diffused light. In revealing

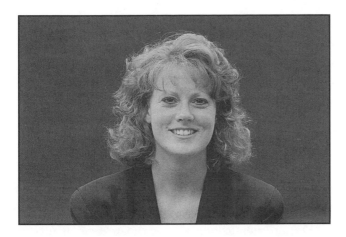

REVEALING LIGHT

light, the shadows are evenly dispersed around the subject. There is no apparent direction or distinguishable source of light. The subject is "revealed" in all its form, with a softened sense of texture, volume, and detail. This can be a very desirable type of light, especially when using color film. Don't be just a "sunny day" photographer.

▼

Color film often gives its best results under revealing light conditions.

The redwood forest under revealing light would be approachable. The surface shadows would be softened, yet there would still be texture and volume.

The subject matter, redwood trees, has been the same in all these examples, but you can sense how very different the side-lit redwood trees were from the back-lit redwoods. The direction of light affects the impact of the photograph and our interpretation. The subject was the same "redwood forest." It was the light that made the difference.

Matching the light to the purpose is important for success. If an architect wants a photograph that shows a building's form and volume, a strong side light would be the appropriate choice. The architect would want to avoid showing the building in front light.

If you wanted to show the beauty of ripples on a sandy beach or the undulating patterns of freshly fallen, wind-blown snow, then you would seek back light, in order to capture texture. Front light would be avoided here, too.

How we see and choose the light to photograph our subject can make the difference between a photograph and a snapshot. You must be sensitive to how light strikes that subject at that moment.

Photography is not the capturing of subject matter on film, but the etching of light in silver. It is the light that is your medium. Light is the mordant, silver the ground.

METER CONTROL

If you understand how your exposure meter works, then you can master all lighting situations. Whether the meter is built in or hand held, if you understand how it works, you will be able to use your camera in difficult lighting situations, conditions where your meter is apt to choose an inappropriate exposure. With knowledge you will be able to overcome and correct for the proper exposure.

18% Reflectance

All the various meter systems average the light entering its sensor to determine the f-stop and shutter speed combination. In a range from pitch black to absolute white, the average tone reproduced in a print represents a middle gray. This mid-gray has been determined to be 18% light reflectance. No matter what type of metering system your camera employs, all meters average light to the mid-point of the photographic gray scale, which is 18% reflectance.

▼
mid-gray =18% light reflectance

(You might expect that the mid-point of the gray scale would be 50% reflectance, but 50% reflectance is a very light gray.)

Zone System Terminology

At this point we need to extend our vocabulary to more easily understand how to further control the camera. The language we use is called "zone system" terminology, and it allows us to describe subjective photographic information.

The "zone system" approach to photography most commonly used today is Minor White's interpretation of Ansel Adams' zone system. While we will only be using the language of the zone system, many advanced photographers use the "zone system of exposure and development" to control and master other technical aspects of the medium. Critics of the system feel it is too exact and laborious. *But, the language of the zone system is remarkably clear and understandable, and will allow us to put to creative use all we know.* This is important for both color and black and white photography.

DIAGRAM 21

CONTINUOUS TONE GRAY SCALE

Now, let's divide that scale into ten different sections, or zones. Each zone has a darker and a lighter side to it, since it is a continuous tone scale. The mid-point of each zone is what is represented in the Zone Scale below:

DIAGRAM 22

ZONE SYSTEM SCALE

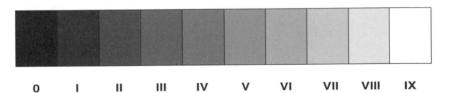

| 0 | I | II | III | IV | V | VI | VII | VIII | IX |

Let's discuss photography in terms of this pitch black to absolute white continuous tone scale. We use Roman numerals to "describe" zones, and any object in a photograph can be ascribed to these zones. (See Chart 11, pg. 70.)

USING THE ZONE SYSTEM

The zone system is an effective means of gaining creative control. But in order to fully control the camera you must be aware of two concepts which are the foundation for understanding creative control.

Two concepts necessary for understanding creative control. First, the relationship between stops is either halves or doubles, and, second, the meter averages light to the mid-point of the gray scale, Zone V, 18% reflectance.

One Zone = One Stop

Each zone is one stop away from the next one in exposure; each zone is twice as much light or half as much light as the zone next to it. Once you understand the interrelationship between stops and zones, control is yours. A one-stop change in exposure is a change of one zone. Two stops = two zones.

Your camera's meter system expects you to include in the photograph a range of dark and

CHART 11

DESCRIPTION OF ZONE VALUES

ZONE	DESCRIPTIVE PROPERTIES (PRINT)
O	*Absolute black* (the darkest the photographic paper can get).
I	*Black* (hint of tone, but no texture).
II	*Darkest gray* (e.g., deep shadows, just perceptible texture in the black).
III	*Darker gray* (e.g., full shadow detail and texture, dark clothing).
IV	*Dark gray* (e.g., average dark green foliage, very dark skin in indirect light, or white skin in deep shadow).
V	***18% reflectance. Middle gray*** (e.g., brown or dark skin, denim jeans).
VI	*Light gray* (e.g., average white skin, snow in shade).
VII	*Lighter gray* (e.g., blue sky, side-lit snow or sand).
VIII	*Lightest gray* (e.g., bright cement, white paint, bright hazy sky, bright snow).
IX	*Paper white* (e.g., spectacular high-lights, no texture).

light subjects on either side of this "average" mid-gray. It will take the light from the dark areas and the light from the bright areas, blend them together, and give an f-stop/shutter speed combination that will match Zone V. When the shot is taken and the lens sharpens the details, those objects that are darker than Zone V will record darker and those objects that are lighter than Zone V will record lighter, based upon that midpoint. The meter is calibrated only to give an exposure to match a Zone V.

▼

The meter is calibrated to give an expo- sure to match Zone V.

Obviously there will be problems when the scene you wish to photograph doesn't conform to the "average" situation. The meter cannot sense when the situation isn't average. If you want to

0	5 stops less exposure than Zone V	
I	4 stops less exposure than Zone V	
II	3 stops less exposure than Zone V	
III	2 stops less exposure than Zone V	**—**
IV	1 stop less exposure than Zone V	
V	**18% REFLECTANCE. MIDDLE GRAY.**	
VI	1 stop more exposure than Zone V	
VII	2 stops more exposure than Zone V	**+**
VIII	3 stops more exposure than Zone V	
IX	4 stops more exposure than Zone V	
X*	5 stops more exposure than Zone V	

CHART 12

INTER- RELATIONSHIP OF ZONES AND STOPS

*Zone X and higher are possible to record on film, but they are not visible in a print.

photograph a solid white wall, for example, you have to consider your purpose and make adjust- ments accordingly. Remember, the meter is calibrated and designed to take whatever light is coming into its sensor and average the light that enters to a mid-gray, 18% reflectance.

How to Make "Zone Placement" Corrections

1. ▶   *On the first frame of a roll of film, shoot a close-up detail of a solid black wall. Fill the entire frame with the black wall. Take the shot with any f-stop and shutter speed combination the camera suggests. (You're not concerned with choice of shutter speed or the f-stop. The subject is not moving and there is no depth-of-field to a flat surface.)*

    The camera's meter system expects to average a range of tones. It has no mechanism for calculating a monotone situation. It takes the light reflected off the black wall and averages it to the midpoint Zone V, to determine an exposure. The photograph will match a perfect Zone V tone; i.e., it will be gray and not black.

    This example shows that you can receive an improper exposure *for a subject* from an accurate, functioning meter. The wall in the photograph was reproduced as a Zone V middle-gray, because the meter did its job well! Clearly, there are situations that require the photographer's intervention.

2. ▶   *Based on our knowledge of how meters work, we need to make a correction. If we want the close-up photo of the black wall to be a barely perceptible textured black, as it really is, then we want to reproduce it in Zone II. To do that, we need to close down from what the camera believes it should be — letting in 3 stops less light.*

    Corrections can be made on either the f-stop or the shutter speed scale (or on a combination of f-stop and shutter speed). We must have 3 stops less light striking the film, in order to render the wall in Zone II.

    Zone V to Zone II   = 3 Zones Less Light
    3 Stops Less Light = 3 Zones Less Light

3. ▶   *On frame #3 of the same role of film, you want a photograph of a white wall. Meter the wall and use the combination it gives. Again, using the combination the meter gives you, you will end up with another middle-gray, Zone V photograph. In fact, you won't be able to tell the difference between*

*frame #1 and frame #3. Both the photograph of
the black wall and the photograph of the white
wall will be Zone V mid-gray walls. Again, your
meter has performed correctly. It gave everything
18% reflectance.*

In order to make the white wall in the photograph white, with a slight hint of texture, you
would want the white wall in the photograph
reproduced in Zone VIII. Therefore, you must
override the meter by letting in 3 stops more light
then the meter system says it needs! The correction of 3 stops could be made on either the f-stop
or the shutter speed, or on a combination of
f-stop and shutter-speed modes.

Overriding the Meter

The meter system must be corrected by
overriding the designated exposure. *The camera
must be set on manual and not any of the
Automatic (A) modes,* which include: Aperture-
priority (AP), Shutter-speed priority (SP), Automatic (A), or Program (P). Remember, these are
all types of "automatic" settings for averaging to
Zone V. If your camera is set to any of these
modes when you try to make a correction by
opening or closing the f-stops, the camera will
automatically counter that adjustment on the
shutter speed scale. Likewise, if you try to correct
with the shutter speeds, the camera will
counter that move by readjusting the f-stops
back to an exposure equivalent to the original
reading. The camera will automatically return
the exposure to Zone V, which is an incorrect
exposure for that subject.

With "automatic" cameras, you must *manually* set the f-stop and shutter-speed the camera
suggested in its automatic mode. On a manual
camera, find the suggested setting. Next, make
the correction. The meter system will blink, flash,
or not align, somehow trying to convince you not
to take the shot. It wants to get back to neutral,
Zone V, but *you know* you need to override what
it is telling you in order to make a proper exposure! You can't trust the meter to give you a proper

exposure. You can only trust the meter to give you Zone V.

Have you ever photographed someone indoors in front of a window? Did you end up with a silhouette? That's because you made an exposure at the indicated meter reading, rather than thinking through the problem at hand.

▶ *Here is what happened: Light entered the meter from the window behind the person. There was more light coming into the meter from the window than there was reflecting off the person within the room. When the meter averaged the scene to Zone V, it made the window, the dominant source of light, reproduce at Zone V or VI. The person, who should have been in Zone VI (if white skinned), reproduced in Zone II or III, looking like a silhouette.*

▶ *Here is how to control the situation: You know the white skin should be in Zone VI. Get close to the person and take a meter reading off her face. Don't allow the meter to point into the window light. The meter will give you an f-stop and shutter-speed combination that will make the skin of the face Zone V. (The meter always averages the light to Zone V.) Since you know the skin should be Zone VI, you open up, or let in, one stop more light than the meter has determined. The skin will now be in Zone VI. If you choose to have the skin reproduce darker, you can take the reading of the skin and make no correction, leaving the skin in Zone V. Now, go back to your original position and reframe the composition with the window.* Once one tone is set, all other tonalities are correct in relationship to it. *If the skin is correct, everything else has to be right, too.*

Knowing how the meter works allows you to figure out what the meter is doing and correct for unusual situations. You'll no longer get troublesome results with no clue as to why your photographs have poor exposure. Single-toned subjects, like snowscapes, or subjects heavily back-lighted, like an interior shot of someone at a bright window, will no longer be a cause for concern. For unusual conditions this "zone placement" *metering correction system will be invaluable.*

Review:
Go up to the subject and meter a single tone. The camera will determine an exposure, placing that tone in Zone V. Correct that single tone as necessary, by overriding the camera. Go back to your original location to compose and take the picture.

You may find that it is time consuming and intrusive to take a close-up meter reading on a single tone, correct that tone by placing it in the proper zone, and then walk back to compose the picture. In most general lighting situations you may wish to utilize light direction correction.

LIGHT DIRECTION CORRECTION

Light direction correction is a useful method when you want to meter from the camera position. No corrections are necessary and you will have excellent results using the exposure indicated by your meter, except in cases of back light.

Photographers who do their own printing find that the following corrections give them slightly better negatives to print from, by rendering a little more detail in the shadows. Others feel that the corrections make negligible difference and therefore are not worth the time or effort. But all agree that the corrections are necessary for back light.

The corrections range from no increase for front light, to a ½ stop increase in exposure for side light, usually 1 to 2 stops increase for back light (1½ stops is a popular choice to correct underexposure in back light), and up to a 1 stop increase for revealing light.

For slide film (called "positive" film, "reversal" film, or "chromes"), no corrections should be made except for back light, with only an increase of ½ to 1 stop of exposure.

All these corrections increase exposure, letting in more light. This is accomplished by using a slower shutter speed or by opening to a larger f-stop aperture (a smaller f-number). Correcting with the f-stop affects the depth-of-field, and correcting with the shutter speed affects motion or movement. Corrections can also be made using the exposure compensation dial.

Front Light (0)

In front light, a general overall meter reading is accurate, no matter what the intensity of the light. The contrast range of the scene falls within the "zones" capable of being recorded on film.

Side Light (+½ stop optional)

When the subject is in side light, most photographers go with the meter reading. But some like to increase the exposure by +½ stop, in order to slightly increase the shadow detail. On most cameras this is accomplished on the f-stop scale, because one can't set shutter speeds between stops. F-stops can be set anywhere between the stops. Some digital cameras have the ability to set shutter speeds between stops.

Back Light (+1½ stops necessary)

Take the meter reading and open up with 1 to 2 stops more light. Some cameras have a back-light switch that automatically increases the exposure 1½ stops.

Recall the back-lit redwood tree example on page 66. Without a correction, the trees would be dark, without texture, uninviting. You have to decide how much of a correction to make, how much of a silhouette you want. Opening up 1½ to 2 stops might be too much of a correction, making the background overly bright and washed out, though it allows detail in the subject. You might want to compromise and increase the exposure a little, maybe just a stop. This is your creative decision.

Revealing Light (+1 stop optional)

This is a broad source of light, without harsh shadows, which easily falls within the contrast range of films. Most photographers don't bother making a correction here. Those that do, open up no more than +1 stop increase in exposure.

Zone Placement and Light Direction Review

Walk up to the person, take a meter reading off her face, and place the Zone V reading in the appropriate zone for her skin. Then return to your position to compose and take the shot.

Stay at the camera position you have chosen for the photograph and take the meter reading as you normally would. Now, open an additional 1½ stops to the suggested exposure in order to prevent the person from becoming a silhouette.

You now know two ways to approach the problem of photographing someone standing at a bright window: zone placement correction and light direction correction. Use one method or the other. Do not combine the two systems.

THE FLASH

"Sync Speed"

When using flash, a focal plane shutter is limited to the *specific* maximum shutter speed for that camera, usually ⅟₆₀ or ⅟₁₂₅ (a few are as fast as ⅟₂₅₀). This maximum speed is called the flash synchronization or *"sync speed"* of the camera. Shutter speeds that are *slower* than the "sync speed" can always be used. But using a "sync speed" faster than designated will produce photographs with part of the frame pitch black and the remainder properly exposed. This is because, at speeds faster than the "sync speed," the window opening between the two curtains is never fully uncovered. Leaf (iris) shutters allow the use of *any* shutter speed for flash photography. There is no "sync speed" to worry about, since light strikes the entire frame as soon as the shutter starts opening.

sync speed

On many cameras and on most older cameras, you must manually adjust the shutter speed to the "sync speed" of your camera. These cameras have an "X," lightning bolt symbol, or distinct color differentiation to designate the "sync speed" for that camera.

Dedicated Flash

Many cameras today have "dedicated" flash units that automatically adjust the camera to the "sync speed" when the flash unit is attached, or, if the flash is built into the camera, when the flash is activated.

Flash Exposure

If you have a very old camera, you might have a choice of M, MP, or X synchronization. Make sure the X terminal and setting are used. The M and MP synchronizations are for flashbulbs no longer in use today. Once the shutter speed is set to the "sync speed" of the camera, the only control needed for proper exposure is the f-stop.

Manual Flash Exposure

Flash unit manufacturers provide specific "Guide Numbers" for each unit, usually listed on the "specifications" page of the instruction manual. This "Guide Number" varies according to the film ISO. Focus on the subject, and divide that distance (shown on the foot/meter scale) into the guide number. The closest f-stop setting or ½ stop setting to that number is the f-stop that should be used.

$$\frac{\textit{Guide Number (G.N.)}}{\textit{flash-to-subject distance}} = \textit{f-stop}$$

Most flash units have a flash calculator dial on the back of the unit. Set the ISO into the calculator, find the flash-to-subject distance, and read the f-stop that aligns with that distance.

Auto-Thyristor

Most flash units have thyristor circuits, which are sensors that receive light from the flash reflected off the subject, and automatically adjust the flash duration for a proper exposure. Each thyristor setting allows the flash to properly light a scene according to the distance the flash has to reach. One setting might allow the flash to light an object anywhere from 3–45 feet, a different thyristor setting from 2–15 feet. You can determine the distance the subject is from the camera by focusing on the subject and looking on the foot/meter scale on the lens. Your subject must fall within the range you've set. You may find that more than one auto-thyristor setting is possible for a given shot. The smaller the f-stop you choose, the less distance the flash will be able to throw its light, but the greater the depth-of-field will be. Thyristors work perfectly when the flash is aimed directly at the subject.

Bounce Flash

Many good flash units allow the head of the flash to tilt up or swing to the side, allowing you to "bounce the flash" — reflect it off a secondary surface before striking the subject. This technique softens the light and reduces contrast between highlights and shadows.

$$\frac{\textit{Guide Number (G.N.)}}{\textit{flash to reflecting surface to subject distance}} = \textit{f-stop + open 1 stop}$$

Manual Correction. To determine the flash-to-subject distance with bounce flash, or the total distance the flash has to travel, calculate the distance of the flash to the reflective surface (ceiling) to the subject. Then use either the calculator wheel or the Guide Number formula. In both cases, open up +1 stop more than the f-stop recommended to allow for light absorption.

Thyristor Correction. Experience has shown that when bouncing flash, you should open the lens f-stop 1 to 2 stops more than if it were a direct flash, even though you have a thyristor that supposedly corrects for bounce. The degree of correction depends on how high and how absorbent your ceiling is. A black ceiling would need more than the additional stop of a white reflective ceiling, for example. And a ceiling that's 8 feet away would need less additional light than one at 16 feet away. When bouncing flash, you might expect the thyristor to compensate, since it's going to take the light a little longer to strike the ceiling, then the subject, then return to the sensor. But with most flash systems, correction is needed. The more vertical the bounce, the farther away something is, or the more absorbent the bounce surface, the more light you'll have to let in. Do some simple tests with your flash. Take some bounce flash shots of a subject without a correction and then with a +1 f-stop correction. If a dark reflective surface or large flash-to-subject distance is used, test +1 and +2 f-stop increases. The results you get can serve to guide you in the future.

Through-the-Lens (TTL) Flash Metering

A dedicated through-the-lens (TTL) flash system senses the amount of light at the film plane. When the proper quantity of light is "read" off the film itself, the sensor shuts off the flash. The camera must be "dedicated" for TTL to allow a TTL flash to be used. This system allows extremely accurate flash photography, especially when doing "close-ups." When using a "zoom" lens or different focal length lenses, or when using bounce-flash or lens filters, the photographer must make a slight correction to manual and automatic flash photography. TTL solves all those problems, and no corrections are necessary. With "automatic" (thyristor) flash, the sensor is on the flash unit, or possibly the camera body. With TTL, the sensor is at the film, where it gives the most accurate exposure possible.

Red Eye

A phenomenon called red eye occurs in low light with color film and direct flash. Since there is significant pupillary eye dilation in low light, a direct flash will reflect off the retinal blood vessels in the back of the eye. This reflection records in the photograph as red spots or flares. Because their pupils are naturally larger, certain animals, like dogs, will exhibit more obvious red eye. The darker the environment, the greater the potential for red eye, because of greater pupil dilation.

To help prevent red eye, simply increase the ambient light in the room by turning on more lights. The pupils will naturally become smaller, thereby decreasing the red eye effect. You can also try asking the subject to look away from the lens. The most popular remedy, however, is to bounce the flash off the ceiling or a side wall to give a diffused light. Direct flash creates red-eye.

Flash Shadows

One way to deal with harsh shadows cast on a wall behind the subject is to have that subject stand away from the wall. The farther away the subject is from the background's reflective surface, the more diffused the shadow will be. A more effective remedy is to bounce the flash off a wall or ceiling, so the light is more diffuse, has less contrast, and strikes the subject indirectly, giving a more pleasing and natural look.

Flash-Fill

Flash-fill is a technique used in outdoor photography to supplement available daylight. It is helpful when the subject is in deep shade, under a heavy, overcast sky, or strongly back-lit or side-lit. By properly balancing the flash exposure one or two stops less bright than the available daylight, texture and detail in the subject become fully visible.

For both automatic and manual flash units, there are various methods that can be employed for flash-fill. You will need to experiment with your specific flash unit to determine a working

FLASH-FILL

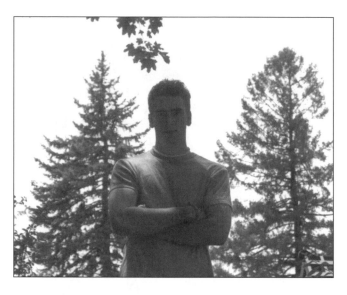

daylight exposure

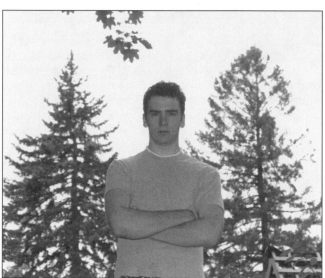

flash-fill

method for flash-fill. However, there is one sure method for achieving a proper sun-to-flash ratio with any camera, which is to set the flash unit to "manual." First, take a meter reading and set the camera to the proper f-stop for a sunlight exposure, using the sync speed as the shutter speed (e.g., f/11 at ⅟₆₀). Next, determine the required flash-to-subject distance. Since the fill should be one-stop less bright than the sunlight, choose one f/stop larger (e.g., f/8) and divide it into the guide number (G.N.) of your particular flash unit (e.g., G.N. 80 / f/8 = 10, meaning the flash unit must be 10 feet from the subject). If this distance is unsuitable and the flash must be closer to the subject, use layers of tissue or handkerchief to reduce the light output.

Some flash units have a variable output feature (½, ¼, ⅛, etc.) for manual operation. If you have variable output, put the flash at the distance called for by the f/stop of the original sunlight exposure and set the flash to half power. Remember, always shoot at the original reading for the sunlight exposure.

FILTERS

Filters control and modify light before it strikes the film. There are filters for black and white and for color film, and a few can be used for both. Most filters are made of glass and screw onto the front of the lens. There are also dyed gelatin filters called "gels." This type of system uses a separate   *gels* filter holder that attaches to the front of the lens, allowing for an easy exchange of gels. Although gels are less expensive, they are more fragile, scratch easily, and are not easily cleaned.

The size of the filter mount varies with the size of the lens. Rather than buy a set of filters for all the lenses you own, however, you can buy the largest diameter filter needed and then use inexpensive *adapter rings* to secure the larger filters to   *adapter rings* the smaller filter mounts.

Standard Filters for All Films

Haze, Polarizing, and Neutral Density filters can be used with all films, both black and white and color.

Haze Filters. Haze, Skylight, and Ultraviolet (UV)   *haze* filters are often sold as "protection" filters. They are clear and offer protection to the front surface of the lens. But if you use a lens cap, as most of us do, why would you also need a clear filter?

Only about 90% of the light passes through a clear filter. Furthermore, a clear filter is an inexpensive piece of glass that might even degrade the image.

There is too much fear instilled in us concerning the front surface of a lens. In fact, if you were to slightly scratch the front surface of your lens and then photograph with it, you would not see the scratch or notice any light-scattering effect in the photograph. The scratch is too close to the lens for it to be focused. Repeated scratching *would* deteriorate the image, but a light scratch or two is virtually impossible to detect.

These filters should be used only for their specific purpose, not for *constant* protection.

It's a good idea to use a UV or skylight filter if you're going to be photographing on water, or near the ocean. Moisture can seep behind the front element and fog the lens. Moisture can also loosen the glues that secure the lens elements in place. Both salt spray and oils from fingerprints on a lens can deteriorate the outer lens coating that helps improve both image contrast and color purity.

Color photographic film is sensitive to ultraviolet light, which is scattered by atmospheric haze. Ultraviolet light has almost no effect on black and white films. With color film there will be a faint blue cast to the image on overcast days or in shadows. A clear (sometimes yellow tinted) "haze" filter *UV filter* called a UV filter will slightly reduce the amount of UV light affecting the film, and the slightly pinkish skylight filter will "warm" the overly bluish cast caused by the ultraviolet light. Neither of these filters has any effect on black and white film. Some filters aren't even designated "UV" or "Skylight," *skylight filter* but are simply called generic "Haze" filters.

Polarizing Filter. The energy waves of light travel in all directions. When they strike reflective, nonmetallic surfaces (like water, glass, dust, or most any smooth surface), they reflect off in one direction. This reflected light is called "polarized light." A polarizing filter can be thought of as

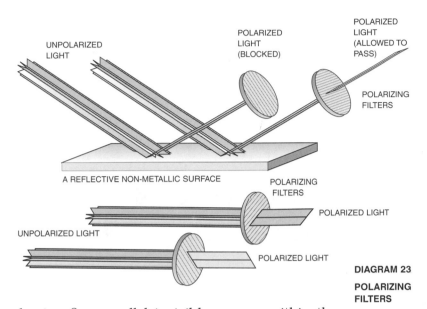

UNPOLARIZED LIGHT

POLARIZED LIGHT (BLOCKED)

POLARIZED LIGHT (ALLOWED TO PASS)

POLARIZING FILTERS

A REFLECTIVE NON-METALLIC SURFACE

POLARIZING FILTERS

UNPOLARIZED LIGHT

POLARIZED LIGHT

POLARIZED LIGHT

DIAGRAM 23

POLARIZING FILTERS

having fine parallel invisible screens within the glass. This filter can be rotated when it is attached to the lens. By rotating the filter, you allow polarized light to travel through the filter or you block it, depending on whether the screens are parallel or perpendicular to the polarized light. Reflections from a store window for example, can virtually be eliminated, revealing the display within. Sometimes you may find that surface reflection or "noise" can add to the impact of a photograph. You decide what you want to show the viewer. It's your creative choice.

Remember, to block or admit polarized light, you must look through the lens and rotate the filter. If you have an SLR this will be easy, since you're looking through the filter. With a rangefinder, however, you have to put the filter up to your eye, mark the orientation you want, and then place it on the lens, readjusting it to that orientation.

With distant scenes and landscapes, light sometimes reflects off atmospheric water vapor, which decreases contrast and creates haze. The polarizing filter can cut through this haze in B/W, darken a blue sky, and, with color film, produce color that is richer, deeper, more pure.

POLARIZING FILTER

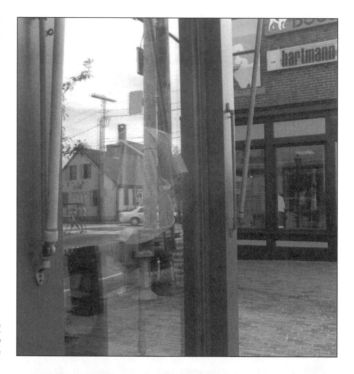

Unpolarized window display

Polarized window display

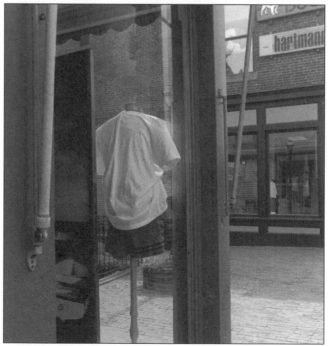

With landscapes, maximum polarization occurs when the camera is at a 90 degree angle to the sun. When a polarizing filter is used to remove reflections, a 30 degree angle to the reflecting surface gives the best results.

The filter factor for a polarizing filter is usually 2.5 or an increase of +1⅓ f-stop. If metering is done through the lens, a correction is automatically made and should be fairly accurate. (See Filter Factor, pg. 92.)

There are two types of polarizing filters: the standard "linear" filter and the more expensive "circular" filter. Most autofocus camera systems *must* use the "circular" polarizer. If your camera uses a beamsplitter or has a semisilvered mirror to determine exposure (as in most autofocus systems), photosensors will receive an improper amount of light through the "linear" polarizer, resulting in improper exposure and possibly poor focus.

Neutral Density Filter. Neutral density filters absorb evenly the wavelengths of all light, without affecting color balance, and therefore reduce the amount of light that reaches the film. They are used in bright light situations, where a slower shutter speed or larger aperture can be used. A 0.15 ND filter reduces light by ½ stop; 0.30 ND reduces light by 1 stop; 0.60 ND reduces light by 2 stops; 0.90 ND reduces light by 3 stops.

CHART 13

NEUTRAL DENSITY FILTERS

NEUTRAL DENSITY AND POLARIZING FILTERS			
NEUTRAL DENSITY (ND)	FILTER COLOR	FILTER FACTOR	F-STOP INCREASE
ND .15	GRAY	1.3	+½
ND .3	GRAY	2	+1
ND .6	GRAY	4	+2
ND .9	GRAY	8	+3
POLARIZING FILTER	GRAY	2.5	+1⅓

**FILTERS FOR
BLACK AND
WHITE FILM**

**(RED BARN,
GREEN ROOF,
BLUE SKY)**

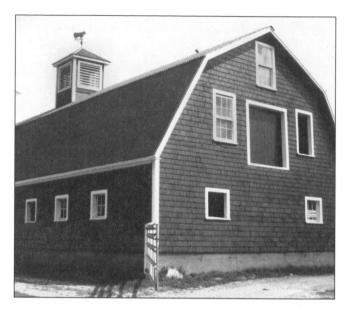

No filter

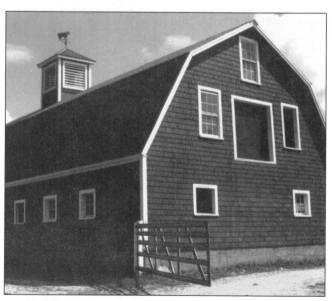

Yellow filter

Filters for B/W Film

Filters are used for contrast control in black and white photographs. They modify tonal relationships selectively, depending on the color of the subject. Basically, a filter lightens its own color and darkens its complementary color.

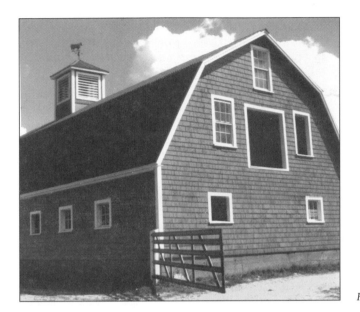

Red filter

Green filter

The most basic B/W filter is a #8 yellow filter. It is used to render a blue sky the "normal" tone in a B/W print. B/W panchromatic film is sensitive to all the colors that the eye is sensitive to *except* for blue. Since, blue reproduces a little lighter than it should, beautiful clouds in the sky (for example) might not appear as prominently as they should in the print. A yellow filter is needed to slightly darken a blue sky. An orange #15 filter would render the blue sky darker than normal, and a red #25 filter would make the sky very dark, with very dramatic, almost threatening clouds. Blue and green filters round out the basic B/W filters. A blue filter darkens red or yellow subject matter, lightens sky, and increases the atmospheric effects of haze. A green filter increases

CHART 14

BLACK AND WHITE FILTERS

WRATTEN FILTER #	FILTER COLOR	FILTER FACTOR		EXPOSURE INCREASE IN"STOPS"	
		DAYLIGHT	(TUNGSTEN)	DAYLIGHT	(TUNGSTEN)
#6	LIGHT YELLOW	1.5		$+\frac{2}{3}$	
#8	**MEDIUM YELLOW**	**2**	**(1.5)**	**+1**	**$(+\frac{2}{3})$**
#9	DARK YELLOW	2	(1.5)	+1	$(+\frac{2}{3})$
#11	YELLOW-GREEN	4		+2	
#13	YELLOW-GREEN	5	(4)	$+2\frac{2}{3}$	(+2)
#15	ORANGE (DEEP YELLOW)	2.5	(1.5)	$+1\frac{1}{3}$	$(+\frac{2}{3})$
#25	**RED**	**8**	**(5)**	**+3**	**$(+2\frac{2}{3})$**
#29	DARK RED	16	(8)	+4	(+3)
#47	BLUE	6	(12)	$+2\frac{2}{3}$	$(+3\frac{1}{2})$
#58	**GREEN**	**8**		**+3**	
#61	DARK GREEN	12		$+3\frac{2}{3}$	

*Note: In Chart 14, the filters listed in bold type are recommended as the first set of B/W filters to own. The #8 filter is highly recommended.

Numbers in parentheses ( ) indicate the filter factor and exposure increase in "stops" necessary for use under "tungsten" light.

the contrast between blue sky and clouds, lightens foliage, darkens flowers and shadows, and accurately renders skin tones. Filter terminology has been standardized with Wratten filter numbers. (Refer to Charts on page 87 and 90.)

Filters for Color Film

Basically, color films are manufactured to respond to a certain color temperature, called the color "balance." The eye adapts well to recognizing colors under all sorts of lighting conditions.

CHART 15

CONVERSION FILTERS FOR COLOR FILM

CONVERSION FILTERS FOR COLOR FILM					
FILTER NUMBER	FILTER COLOR	FILTER FACTOR	EXPOSURE INCREASE IN "STOPS"	LIGHT SOURCE CONVERSION IN DEGREES KELVIN	FOR USE WITH COLOR FILM TYPES
80A	BLUE	4	2	3200 TO 5500	DAYLIGHT
80B	BLUE	3	$1\frac{2}{3}$	3400 TO 5500	DAYLIGHT
85	AMBER	1.5	$\frac{2}{3}$	5500 TO 3400	TYPE A
85B	AMBER	1.5	$\frac{2}{3}$	5500 TO 3200	TUNGSTEN TYPE B

But, film is very exacting. Daylight has a very different "color temperature" for film than light from standard tungsten-filament light bulbs. Daylight is "bluer" and cooler than the "yellow-orange" or warmer light of a bulb. Color films are either "daylight" balanced at 5500K (the most common film used), or "tungsten" balanced at 3200K (Type B) and 3400K (Type A).

There are a few categories of filters for color film: ***Conversion, Light Balancing, and Color Compensating (CC).***

Conversion Filters. Conversion filters are used to adjust the color temperature of the light source, so it matches the color balance of the film.

When daylight film is used indoors without a flash (a flash is considered daylight balanced), and the source of light is standard tungsten lightbulbs, the orange cast of those bulbs produces an unrealistic orange cast in the photograph. You need to use an 80A filter to convert the color temperature of the light so it matches the film. Likewise, if a "tungsten" balanced film is used outdoors, the photographs come out disturbingly blue. An 85B filter is needed to use "tungsten" film outdoors.

Light Balancing Filters. Fluorescent lights create a different problem, for they emit a discontinuous light from the spectrum. Fluorescent filters exist to correct the unusually blue-green cast that the light produces in color film (FL-D for daylight film and FL-B for tungsten film). Other light balancing filters, 81 series amber filters, can warm the excessive blue in high UV scenes like snow, high altitude, water, and landscapes. Conversely, bluish 82 series filters can be used to "cool" or eliminate the warm quality of early morning or late afternoon light.

Color Compensation Filters. These filters are generally used by professionals for very precise fine tuning in color. Filters exist in red, green, blue, cyan, magenta, and yellow. Each affects specific colors, heightening or reducing their intensity. Certain "professional" films need this type of color correction to achieve perfect balance. The manufacturers suggest adding specific CC filters, in the instruction sheet they pack with the film.

Filter Factor

Many filters absorb so much light that adjustments must be made in order to achieve proper exposure. Many photographers just meter through the lens with the filter in place, and in most situations that works just fine. Unfortunately, with denser filters the exposure might not be accurate, due to the altered spectral sensitivity of the meter in relationship to the spectral sensitivity of the film. In those cases the filter factor correction is recommended. First, meter without the filter, then place the filter on the lens and adjust the exposure by the filter factor. The factor will differ depending on whether the filter is used under daylight or tungsten (artificial) light. The filter factor is a simple multiplication of the given exposure.

Example:
A given exposure of ⅟₅₀₀ and a filter factor of 2 would be ⅟₅₀₀ x 2 = ⅟₂₅₀. In other words, a filter factor of 2 is equal to an increase in exposure of one stop. That increase of one stop could also have been made on the f-stop scale, instead.

Note:
Clear filters need no adjustment. Metering through light-colored *filters and polarizing filters also gives excellent results. Metering through dark filters, like a 25 red, will often lead to underexposure because of the absorption of blue light by the filter.*

CHART 16
FILTER FACTORS

IF FILTER FACTOR IS:	INCREASE EXPOSURE THIS MANY STOPS:
1	0
1.2	⅓
1.5	⅔
2	1
2.5	1⅓
3	1⅔
4	2
5	2⅓
6	2⅔
8	3
10	3⅓
12	3⅔
16	4
32	5

BATTERIES

There are five types of batteries used in photographic systems: lithium, alkaline, silver oxide, zinc oxide, and mercury. Lithium batteries rarely leak, and some camera systems require them. But lithium batteries can sometimes cause improper exposure due to voltage fluctuation. Alkaline and mercury batteries tend to leak. Silver oxide batteries are the most reliable in cold weather and last longer than alkaline and mercury batteries.

Mercury batteries are no longer manufactured in the United States and few of today's cameras use them. For the time being mercury batteries are still imported, but they are expensive. Cameras that rely on 625 (PX13) mercury batteries can use zinc oxide as a direct replacement, or be retrofitted to accept silver oxide. Zinc oxide batteries are very expensive and have a short life. Cameras with a silver oxide retrofit require a one-time recalibration of the meter system because of the voltage difference. There are some who believe that retrofitted cameras have the potential for other camera circuitry problems.

Whether you have a button, AA, AAA, or any specialized photographic battery, you should never touch the battery terminals. Oils from your skin can cause corrosion that affects the electric current. If the batteries have leaked and deteriorated to the point where you see a white "talc" around the gasket or contact points, the battery must be removed immediately. *The battery check may still show the battery to be good.* The constant gaseous leak causes oxidation build-up between the battery contact and the camera body contact points. If you see a white powder, you can be sure the metal contact points in the battery compartment are corroding. It is more common though, for a battery to look fine but fail to deliver a current. Simple battery problems are the major cause of most trips to the camera repair shop.

A reputable camera repair shop will show you how to deal with oxidation build-up, but here's how to do it. Remove the batteries, and rub all the contact points, including the top and bottom of the batteries, with an eraser. You can use the eraser on a pencil, but the coarse white eraser on the back of a ballpoint pen is even better. On highly corroded contacts, try using an emery board. There is a very good chance the problem will be corrected. Oxidation build-up from the previous batteries occasionally prevents the new batteries from making solid contact. By polishing clean the contact points, the oxidation chemical build-up is removed, and the current can flow. *At every battery change* (which, to play safe, should be once a year), *clean the contact points.* And while you're at it, also *clean off the contact point on the hot shoe.*

If the batteries in your camera should go dead when you're on location or in the field, and new ones are unavailable, try removing the "dead" batteries and cleaning all metal contact points on the batteries and on the contacts with an eraser (or buff hard with cloth material). Replace the batteries, and you may be surprised to find you can get more life from them.

THREE TIPS FOR HAND-HELD SHOTS

In general, the longer the focal length of a lens, the more difficult it is to hand hold it. Remember, a telephoto lens magnifies everything—it magnifies the size of an object and it magnifies camera movement. It's like good binoculars. No matter how steady you hold them, when you look through them, you will notice that the scene vibrates as though in an earthquake.

Since any camera movement affects the sharpness of the photograph, it is critical to find a position in which you are most steady. Some photographers hold the camera with one hand under and supporting the lens; others hold onto the sides of the camera. Here are several tips to help you prevent camera movement.

Body Tripod   ◀ 1.

Always hold your arms so that your elbows are down against your chest. When your arms are out to the side, the lack of support creates muscle tension, which can result in minor camera movement. If you create a tripod with your body, your camera will be held extremely steady. Place your elbows against your chest and the eyepiece of the viewfinder firmly against your skull. If you wear glasses, press the viewfinder firmly against your eyeglass lens, pressing the frames back until no further movement is possible.

Breathing   ◀ 2.

The second factor is breathing. This is most important. You should release the shutter after you exhale. Before inhaling, your body is at its calmest and therefore the camera can be held steadiest. You never want to photograph while holding your breath, or with your lungs full.

Shutter Release Squeeze   ◀ 3.

The third factor is the release of the shutter. It is most important to slowly squeeze the button even after you hear it release. Do not jerk your finger down and up.

If you follow these three tips, you should be able to hand hold a shot at a slower speed than any book suggests. There is an old rule of thumb: "Use the shutter speed closest to the focal length of the lens" ($\frac{1}{60}$ for a 50 mm lens; $\frac{1}{125}$ for a 150 mm lens; $1/500$ for a 500 mm lens). If you follow these three suggestions and put the camera directly up against your skull, you probably can hand hold up to *two stops* slower speed. If you wear glasses, you can easily hand hold *one stop* slower than usual. Test it out for yourself—you'll be surprised. You might find you can hand hold the camera at even slower speeds.

If you have trouble holding the camera steady, for whatever reason, use a tripod and a cable release.

LENS AND CAMERA CARE

Many photographers today carry their cameras in small camera bags with special compartments for extra lenses, flash units, film, etc. These padded bags protect the camera from physical shock and the weather.

▶   Avoid storing a camera in excessive heat, as in a car parked in the sun. The heat can cause the lubricants in the camera and lens to seep, causing serious damage.

▶   A short, comfortable neckstrap is highly recommended. The longer the neckstrap, the more the camera will swing and jostle against the body. A dense foam camera strap is highly recommended for comfort .

▶   Never store a manual camera with the shutter cocked.

▶   If a camera is not going to be used for a few months, remove the batteries.

▶   Try not to touch the surface contact point of the batteries when placing them in the camera or flash. The oil from fingers can cause corrosion of the battery, affecting the proper flow of electric current.

▶   In damp environments, don't store cameras in plastic bags for long periods of time. You can use plastic bags for storage for short periods, if you place moisture-absorbing silica gel packets with the equipment.

▶ Use a rubber syringe to blow dust from a lens or camera body, or use "environmentally safe" compressed gas sparingly. These cans of "air" might be ozone safe, but their warning labels indicate that they contain "toxic vapors."

▶ Do not clean a lens unless it is very dirty. To clean a lens, wet a piece of lens tissue with lens cleaner, then rub the surface of the lens gently, using a circular motion. Never apply the lens cleaner directly to the surface of the lens. The liquid could seep behind the outer seal and cause condensation within the elements of the lens.

RECIPROCITY FAILURE AND CORRECTION

With very long or very short exposures, the sensitivity of film decreases. There is no longer a reciprocal relationship of exposure time and illuminance to the resulting exposure density on film.

When exposures are longer than 1 second or shorter than $\frac{1}{2000}$ second, most films need an increase in the amount of light striking them in order to obtain the required density for proper exposure. Bracketing, making additional, longer *bracketing* exposures around the suggested exposure, is highly recommended for exposures longer than one second. Exposure compensation for the extremely short, fast exposures can generally be ignored, but for long exposures, correction is definitely needed.

INDICATED EXPOSURE TIME:	OPEN APERTURE:	REDUCE FILM DEVELOPMENT TIME:
1 SEC.	1 STOP	10 %
10 SEC.	2 STOPS	20 %
100 SEC.	3 STOPS	30 %

CHART 17

RECIPROCITY CORRECTIONS FOR BLACK AND WHITE FILM

Each film has its own recommended reciprocity correction. Black and white films are easier to correct because they have one emulsion layer. Color films have three separate emulsion layers. Each of the three layers responds differently to the effects of reciprocity failure. Since specific filtration corrections are needed to compensate for the shifts in color, the film manufacturer's recommendation should be followed. If you want to make an educated guess for color film, bracket around the following suggested corrections for black and white film. (Ideally, the film development time should be reduced, because correcting for reciprocity increases the contrast of film. Shorter film development time reduces contrast. Don't worry if you can't control this.)

RULE OF F/16

An old time rule of thumb states that whenever you are photographing an average scene in direct or overcast light, a good exposure can quickly be made by using f/16 and the reciprocal of the film speed for the shutter speed. Using an ISO 400 film, the shutter would be $\frac{1}{500}$ (closest). Using an ISO 125 film, the shutter speed would be $\frac{1}{125}$ at f/16 or an equivalent. This is obviously gambling and should be your last resort, though it usually will produce fairly good results.

INFRARED PHOTOGRAPHY

Infrared film is sensitive to visible light, as well as to the longer wavelengths of infrared. There is a slight difference between infrared focus and visual focus. Infrared (IR) rays are refracted to a lesser extent than visible light, placing the focus behind the film. To correct for this discrepancy, focus as usual on the subject, then rotate the focusing ring until that indicated distance is set opposite the red IR index on the lens (usually a red dot or line).

PUSHING FILM

"Pushing" film means to intentionally underexpose and overdevelop film, usually to allow for shooting in low-light situations (without flash), or for aesthetic reasons. To push film, adjust the

ISO setting one or two stops higher (faster) than the film calls for. Pushing one stop means under-exposing one-stop; pushing two-stops means underexposing two-stops. The camera will adjust for the higher speed film and therefore require less exposure. For example, to push ISO 400 film one stop, set the ISO to 800. ISO 400 film set to 1600 is pushed two stops.

Some improvement is made to this underexposed film through over-development. The characteristics of pushed film are very poor shadow detail, acceptable mid and high values, and an increase in contrast and grain. Custom labs can usually handle push development of up to two stops.

SUGGESTIONS FOR UNUSUAL AND LOW LIGHT EXPOSURES

Television Screen Photography

With a few precautions, shooting pictures off a television screen or video monitor is quite easy. The only source of light should be the light from the television image. Turn off all lights in the room. Set the camera on a tripod, parallel to the screen. Reduce the contrast of the television image with the contrast control (you want to produce an image that is soft, but with accurate brightness). Set the camera to a shutter speed of $\frac{1}{15}$ or $\frac{1}{30}$, and use the f/stop indicated by the camera. Since a television beam "scans" the screen at $\frac{1}{30}$ of a second, shutter speeds set faster than $\frac{1}{30}$ record a diagonal black band because the beam has not had time to complete its cycle. Longer shutter speeds cause the film to record additional scans, which will create a blur or lack of sharpness. With color film, use a CC40R color correction filter on the lens to counteract the green/blue cast of the television.

Low Light, Firelight, and Moonlight Exposures

The exposures in Chart 18 are estimates. Bracketing is required to get acceptable results. For exposures below one second, you will have to correct for reciprocity failure.

CHART 18

LOW LIGHT EXPOSURES (ESTIMATED)

EXPOSURE*	LOW LIGHT SITUATION
$\frac{1}{60}$	Open fire, campfire (recording flames)
$\frac{1}{15}$	Scene (faces) illuminated by open fire, neon lights, twilight
$\frac{1}{8} - \frac{1}{15}$	Lighted fields (e.g., outdoor sports), brightly lit stage
$\frac{1}{2} - \frac{1}{4}$	Amusement park, fireworks (against dark sky), carnival
1 – 2 SEC	Exterior house lighting, Christmas trees, candlelit scene
	Moonlit landscape (bright enough to produce produce shadows, silhouettes)
2 – 4 MIN	Full
4 – 8 MIN	$\frac{3}{4}$
NA	$\frac{1}{4}$, crescent
	Moon as subject
$\frac{1}{30}$	Full
$\frac{1}{15}$	$\frac{3}{4}$
$\frac{1}{2}$	$\frac{1}{4}$, crescent

* AT F/8 AT ISO 200

Note:
If you use a different f/stop (or shutter speed), either double or halve the exposure time (or f/stop), following the law of reciprocity (e.g., f/8 at $\frac{1}{60}$ = f/11 at $\frac{1}{30}$). If you use a film with a different ISO, a change in the above recommended exposures will be required. For every doubling or halving of the film speed a corresponding change of one stop in exposure is necessary. Doubling the film speed requires one stop less exposure; halving the film speed requires one stop more exposure (e.g., f/8 at $\frac{1}{60}$ with ISO 200 film = f/5.6 at $\frac{1}{60}$ or f/8 at $\frac{1}{30}$ with ISO 100 film).

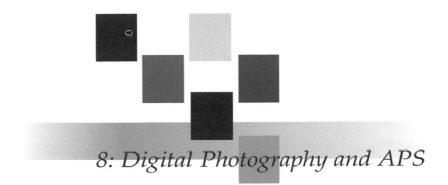

8: Digital Photography and APS

DIGITAL PHOTOGRAPHY

Digital imaging is the latest revolution in still photography. It has had a tremendous impact on a number of photo related fields. Commercial photography and photojournalism were the first areas of photography to feel the change, and the photo-finishing industry will surely be next. It is not uncommon for processed film to be returned as digitized files, and most digital cameras interface with both Macintosh and Windows computer operating systems.

The Digital Camera

Digital cameras come in all sizes and shapes and look remarkably like small-sized compact cameras, point-and-shoot and APS cameras, or high-end 35 mm SLR's. The product appears to be divided into three tiers: low-end amateur (consumer) cameras, more sophisticated and higher-priced "prosumer" models, and 35 mm high-end professional cameras. The higher end cameras tend to have f/stop and shutter speed controls. Digital film backs are another innovation available for medium and large format cameras. They take the place of the traditional film back in these cameras.

Digital cameras usually have most of the following features:

▶ *An autofocus lens.* This lens usually has a short focal length, approximately one-seventh the focal

digital camera

length of a comparable 35 mm camera lens. A 7 mm lens is comparable to a 50 mm normal lens, and a 7–21 mm zoom lens is similar to a 50 –150 mm zoom on a 35 mm camera.

An optical and/or digital zoom lens. The optical zoom is superior because the lens determines how much of the scene actually falls upon the CCD (Charge Coupled Device) chip, filling it with original accurate information. The digital zoom takes the portion of the image that strikes the CCD and digitally enlarges it to fit the entire chip. Interpolated (mathematically calculated) information is used to fill the chip, to plug information into all the pixels. Because there aren't as many true original pixels, the image is inferior to the optical zoom lens. This lens is adjusted by a zoom control.

▼
Film-based cameras will not be obsolete anytime soon, so don't worry about your camera investment.

A connection terminal, or port. This port connects the camera to the computer. Most cameras also have a terminal to allow for direct connection to an external power supply.

A mode dial. This allows the photographer to switch from recording to reviewing, saving, or deleting the digital image.

An optical viewfinder and/or LCD monitor. Used for composing, the LCD allows the photographer to review shots after exposure (but beware, it is a major drain on batteries).

Built-in flash units. These units are common, but not very powerful features of most consumer cameras. They do not have the flash distance of auxiliary flash units on 35 mm cameras.

Additional features. Many digital cameras allow a choice of metering modes, light balance controls, and numerous other capabilities.

CCD (Charge-Coupled Device)—Digital "Film"

CCD

The image acquisition device of all digital cameras is a "chip" or CCD sensor, which con-

verts light into pixels. These pixels are sensitive to   *pixel*
red, green, and blue light. The sensitivity of the
chip is designated with an "equivalent ISO" rating
(for comparison to film). With a regular 35 mm
camera, the photographer can adjust for a variety
of lighting situations by choosing from a range of
film stocks that vary in ISO ratings and are
appropriate to the lighting conditions. However, a
digital camera user is bound by the sensitivity of
the CCD chip in the camera: the chip is the film.
So, cameras with high "equivalent ISO" ratings
have higher sensitivity to low light, and therefore,
more versatility.

Image Resolution

Resolution in a digital camera is the ability
of a chip to record fine detail. The resolution is
described by the quantity of horizontal pixels
multiplied by the number of vertical pixels (e.g.,
1024 x 768). A megapixel camera has a chip of at
least a million pixels. Two-megapixel and three-
megapixel consumer cameras will soon be the
standard. These produce beautifully detailed
prints from photo-quality ink-jet printers. A high
resolution camera is not necessary for viewing
photographs on computer monitors or sending
them over the internet. The resolution of a computer monitor is fairly low, and therefore cannot
show the extremely high resolution produced by
expensive digital cameras.

Image Storage

One of the limiting factors in digital photography is the memory (built-in image storage) of
the camera. On less expensive cameras, the total
number of images is restricted by the built-in
memory. More sophisticated cameras have additional storage, or memory, available on a removable
memory card (storage card.) The digital camera   *memory card*
industry appears to be standardizing with
SmartMedia and CompactFlash cards. Two
other possibilities for storage are floppy disks
(very limited space) and PCMCIA Type I, Type II,
and Type III cards (high capacity).

Image Compression

Since digital images can be extremely large, digital cameras must have the ability to compress the file size to greatly enhance the storage capacity. There are basically two types of compression: *lossy* "lossy" and "lossless." "Lossy" compression saves the greatest amount of space by eliminating some of the pixels that the compression software deems unnecessary or redundant. Therefore, there is some degradation of image quality based on the degree of compression. In digital photography a "lossy" compression method devised by the Joint *JPEG* Photographic Experts Group (JPEG) is the most popular standard in use. JPEG compression first transforms the image data into color and brightness values through a sophisticated mathematical formula. The next stage of JPEG compression determines which information will be discarded. The final step in the compression is the encoding of the information. When the file is reconstituted, the process is reversed, but some of the original image information is sacrificed.

TIFF Tagged Image File Format (TIFF) is another *LZW* popular file format. Through LZW (Lempel-Ziv-Welch) compression, a TIFF file can have a "lossless" compression. This popular "lossless" compression is an algorithm that analyzes repeated pixel sequences and designates a compression code for these combinations, or strings. Simply speaking, the LZW compression scheme encodes the data in an efficient and space-saving manner. As the term suggests, the file can be reconstituted without loss of any information, maintaining quality and detail.

In time, the advantages of the digital camera will make it the dominant tool for capturing visual images. One advantage this camera has is the elimination of the time-consuming chemical development processes for film and prints. Another is the sophisticated software now available for home computers, which allows image enhancement and manipulation. Cropping, color enhancement, contrast control, montage and various other artistic techniques are now available to the photo enthusiast . In addition, photo-quality ink-jet printers can produce prints which are as good as store-processed prints. When an appropriate size file is printed to its ideal image size on fine photographic paper, the results are quite breathtaking. Improvements in the cost and size of various digital storage and retrieval systems, and the ability to transmit a photograph to any other computer or printer in the world within seconds of taking the shot are making digital photography a popular medium.

The technology is growing and will continue to force change. Silver-based photographs consume non-renewable and increasingly scarce resources. The computer will replace the darkroom, and viewing the image on a monitor will be sufficient for many individuals, and those who want paper prints can still produce their own fine quality inkjet photos.

What is most interesting is that the manufacturers of these high-quality digital field cameras are building them around existing high-end 35 mm camera bodies. Photographers still have to know how a camera functions and understand exposure, f/numbers and shutter speeds, metering and exposure. The information in Creative Camera Control is as important to the digital camera user as it is to the silver-based photographer.

ADVANCED PHOTO SYSTEM

The Advanced Photo System (APS) was developed by five photo-industry corporate giants: Nikon, Canon, Kodak, Fuji, and Minolta. This system uses a special film which is 40% smaller than 35 mm film and incompatible with 35 mm cameras. While a single frame of 35 mm film is 24 mm x 36 mm, a single frame of APS film is 17 mm x 30 mm and has a magnetic and optical strip for information. This specially manufactured film must be used in an APS engineered point-and-shoot type camera. More expensive APS cameras have built-in zoom lenses with autofocus capabilities, and built-in flashes. Some manufacturers now offer

APS

high-end APS cameras with interchangeable lenses and f/stop and shutter speed controls.

IX   High-end APS cameras with the Information Exchange (IX) feature magnetically record lighting and scene data on each frame of the film for more accurate lab processing. IX sometimes has a print quantity feature, allowing a print quantity number for a shot at the time of exposure. Printing labs can then automatically print up the designated number of copies during the initial film and print process. Another feature often available in IX is titling of photographs.

APS is clearly marketed to the point-and-shoot amateur. It combines innovative technologies for the camera, film, photofinishing equipment, and image display devices. Most APS cameras allow the photographer to remove film cartridges mid-roll; if the cartridge is reinserted, the camera continues shooting where it left off. Moreover, it combines silver-halide photography with digital information.

C, H, P formats   This camera is simple to operate. The film cartridge has no leader; it only needs to be dropped into the camera. Before shooting each frame the user chooses the desired format: Classic (C), High Definition (H), or Panorama (P). An image mask in the viewfinder shows the chosen format.

index print   After processing, the film is returned in the same cartridge, where it is safely stored. All prints have the time, date, and other coded information stamped on the back of each print, and an "index print" showing all the photos in sequence on the roll. Reprints and enlargements are ordered from the information on the index print, or from information on the back of individual prints. Any of the three print formats can be chosen from any negative after the film has been processed and printed.

The prints can be specified 3½ or 4 inches wide; the length and cropping are determined by the format choice (C, H, or P). The H format uses the full frame and has an aspect ratio of 9:16 (similar to HDTV). The C format has an aspect ratio of 2:3 (similar to 35 mm format) and cuts off some of the left and right side of the full-frame negative. The P format has an aspect ratio of 1:3. It cuts the top and bottom off the full frame to give a panoramic effect, and greatly enlarges the negative that is left. With additional equipment, the APS system allows the film to be viewed on a home TV monitor. Additionally, negatives can be digitized into a home computer with a system film   *film scanner* scanner for further manipulation via graphic and/or image-enhancement software.

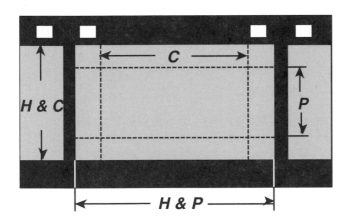

DIAGRAM 24

ADVANCED PHOTO SYSTEM (C), (H), (P) FORMATS

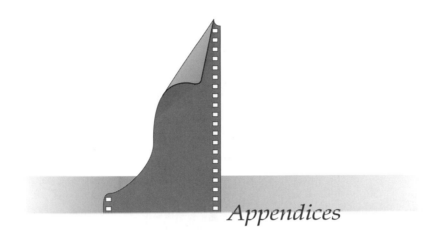

Appendices

ISO	ASA	DIN
4/7°	4	7
6/9°	6	9
10/11°	10	11
12/12°	12	12
16/13°	16	13
20/14°	20	14
25/15°	25	15
32/16°	32	16
40/17°	40	17
50/18°	50	18
64/19°	64	19
80/20°	80	20
100/21°	100	21
125/22°	125	22
160/23°	160	23
200/24°	200	24
250/25°	250	25
320/26°	320	26
400/27°	400	27
500/28°	500	28
640/29°	640	29
800/30°	800	30
1000/31°	1000	31
1600/33°	1600	33
3200/36°	3200	36

◀ **APPENDIX 1**

ISO/ASA FILM SPEED CONVERSION TABLE

6	8	10
12	16	20
25	32	40
50	64	80
100	125	160
200	250	320
400	500	650
800	1000	1250
1600	2000	2500
3200	4000	5000

◀ **APPENDIX 2**

ISO/ASA FILM SPEEDS

Each ISO/ASA film speed number is ⅓ stop faster than the previous one.

APPENDIX 3

F-STOPS

The relationship among f-stops; divided from full into thirds and halves

full

thirds

halves

full	thirds	halves
f / 1.4		
	f / 1.6	
		f / 1.7
	f / 1.8	
f / 2		
	f / 2.2	
		f / 2.4
	f / 2.5	
f / 2.8		
	f / 3.2	
		f / 3.4
	f / 3.5	
f / 4		
	f / 4.5	
		f / 4.9
	f / 5	
f / 5.6		
	f / 6.3	
		f / 6.9
	f / 7	
f / 8		
	f / 9	
		f / 9.8
	f / 10	
f / 11		
	f / 12.5	
		f / 13.5
	f / 14	
f / 16		
	f / 18	
		f / 19.6
	f / 20	
f / 22		
	f / 25	
		f / 27
	f / 28	
f / 32		

BLACK AND WHITE FILMS *(Continuous Tone)*

FILM	ISO	FILM CODE	
EASTMAN KODAK (www.kodak.com)			
Techpan 25 Professional	25		
T-Max 100 Professional	100	TMX	
Plus-X Pan	125	PX	
T-Max 400 Professional	400	TMY	
Tri-X Pan	400	TX	
T-Max 3200 Professional	3200	TMZ	
T400 CN Professional	400	TCN	*C-41 color processing*
High Speed Infrared Film	NA	HIS	*Extended red sensitivity*
FUJI (www.fujifilm.com)			
Neopan 400 Professional	400		
Neopan 1600 Professional	1600		
FORTE (www.forte-photo.com)			
Fortepan 100	100	FP-100	
Fortepan 200	200	FP-200	
Fortepan 400	400	FP-400	
Portraitpan 100	100	PP-100	*not in 35 mm*
AGFA (www.agfa.com)			
Agfapan APX 25 Professional	25		
Agfapan APX 100 Professional	100		
Agfapan APX 200 S	200		*Extended red sensitivity*
Agfapan APX 400 Professional	400		
Scala 200X Professional	200*		*Scala processing lab*
KONICA (www.konica.com)			
Monochrome VX 400	400		*C-41 color processing*
Infrared 750	NA		*Extended red sensitivity*
ILFORD PHOTO (www.ilford.com)			
Pan F plus	50		
FP4 plus	125		
HP5 plus	400		
Delta 100	100		
Delta 400	400		
Delta 3200	3200		
XP2 Super 400	400		*C-41 color processing*
SFX 200	200		*Extended red sensitivity*
CACHET/fappco (www.onecachet.com)			
Macophot UP 100	100		
Macophot UP 400	400		
Maco 820C			*Extended red sensitivity*
POLAROID (www.polaroid.com)			
PolaPan CT	125*		*Needs Polaroid processor*

* B&W Reversal Film

APPENDIX 5 **AMATEUR COLOR PRINT FILMS**

The following charts list two categories of color negative (print) films and color reversal (slide) films: professional and amateur (standard, over-the-counter) films.

Professional films are manufactured under more rigid specifications, with tighter tolerances and narrower latitude.

FILM	ISO	FILM CODE
EASTMAN KODAK (www.kodak.com)		
Gold 100	100	
Gold 200	200	
Royal Gold 100	100	
Royal Gold 200	200	
Royal Gold 400	400	
Royal Gold 1000	1000	
Max 400	400	
Max Zoom 800	800	

FILM	ISO	FILM CODE
FUJI (www.fujifilm.com)		
Fujicolor Superia 100	100	CN
Fujicolor Superia 200	200	CA
Fujicolor Superia X-TRA 400	400	CH
Fujicolor Superia X-TRA 800	800	CZ
Fujicolor Super HG 1600	1600	CU
Fujicolor Superia Reala	100	CS

FILM	ISO	FILM CODE
AGFA (www.agfa.com)		
Agfacolor HDC 100 plus	100	
Agfacolor HDC 200 plus	200	
Agfacolor HDC 400 plus	400	

FILM	ISO	FILM CODE
KONICA (www.konica.com)		
Centuria 100	100	
Centuria 200	200	
Centuria 400	400	
Centuria 800	800	

FILM	ISO	FILM CODE
FERRANIA IMAGING TECHNOLOGIES (www.ferraniait.com) (also sold under private label brands)		
Solaris 100	100	
Solaris 200	200	
Solaris 400	400	
Solaris 800	800	

FILM	ISO	FILM CODE
POLAROID (www.polaroid.com)		
OneFilm 100	100	
OneFilm 200	200	
OneFilm 400	400	
OneFilm Plus	400	
HD 100	100	
HD 200	200	
HD 400	400	

AMATEUR COLOR REVERSAL FILMS   **APPENDIX 6**

FILM	ISO	FILM CODE
EASTMAN KODAK (www.kodak.com)		
Kodachrome 25	25	
Kodachrome 40 Film 5070	40	
Kodachrome 64	64	
Kodachrome 200	200	
Ektachrome Elite II 50	50	
Ektachrome Elite II 100	100	
Ektachrome Elite II 200	200	
Ektachrome Elite II 400	400	
Ektachrome 160 T	160	

FUJI (www.fujifilm.com)		
Fujichrome Sensia II 100	100	RA
Fujichrome Sensia II 200	200	RM
Fujichrome Sensia II 400	400	RH

AGFA (www.agfa.com)		
Agfachrome CT precisa 100	100	
Agfachrome CT precisa 200	200	

FERRANIA IMAGING TECHNOLOGIES		
(www.ferraniait.com)		
(also sold under private label brands)		
Solaris 100	100	
Solaris 400	400	

POLAROID (www.polaroid.com)		
PolaChrome **	40	
PolaChrome HC **	40	

** Needs Polaroid processor

APPENDIX 7   PROFESSIONAL COLOR PRINT FILMS

FILM	ISO	FILM CODE
EASTMAN KODAK (www.kodak.com)		
Supra 100	100	
Supra 400	400	
Supra 800	800	
Portra 100T	100	
Portra 160VC	160	
Portra 160NC	160	
Portra 400VC	400	
Portra 400NC	400	
Portra 800	800	

FILM	ISO	FILM CODE	
FUJI (www.fujifilm.com)			
Fujicolor NPC 160	160	NPC	
Fujicolor NPS 160	160	NPS	
Fujicolor NPL 160	160	NPL	*not in 35 mm*
Fujicolor 400 NPH	400	NPH	
Fujicolor Press 400	400		*20 pack only*
Fujicolor Press 800	800		*20 pack only*
Fujicolor NHG II 800	800	NHG	*not in 35 mm*

FILM	ISO
AGFA (www.agfa.com)	
Agfacolor Ultra 50	50
Agfacolor Optima II Prestige	100
Agfacolor Portrait XPS	160
Agfacolor Optima II Prestige	200
Agfacolor Optima II Prestige	400

FILM	ISO
KONICA (www.konica.com)	
Impressa 50	50
Professional 160	160
Professional 400	400

PROFESSIONAL COLOR REVERSAL FILMS

APPENDIX 8

FILM	ISO	FILM CODE
EASTMAN KODAK (www.kodak.com)		
Kodachrome 25	25	PKM
Kodachrome 64	64	PKR
Kodachrome 200	200	PKL
Ektachrome 64	64	EPR
Ektachrome 64T	64	EPY
Ektachrome E100VS	100	E100VS
Ektachrome E100S	100	E100S
Ektachromo E100SW	100	E100SW
Ektachrome E200	200	E200
Ektachrome 100	100	EPN
Ektachrome 100 Plus	100	EPP
Ektachrome 160 T	160	EPT
Ektachrome 200	200	EPD
Ektachrome 320T	320	EPJ
Ektachrome 400 X	400	EPL
Ektachrome P1600	1600	EPH
Ektachrome Infrared	100/200	EIR
FUJI (www.fujifilm.com)		
Fujichrome Velvia	50	RVP
Fujichrome 64 T Type II	64	RTPII
Fujichrome Astia 100	100	RAP
Fujichrome Provia 100F	100	RDPIII
Fujichrome Provia 400	400	RHP
Fujichrome Provia 1600	1600	RSP
Fujichrome MS 100/1000	100	RMS —————— up to IE 1000 push process
AGFA (www.agfa.com)		
Agfachrome RSX II 50	50	RSX50
Agfachrome RSX II 100	100	RSX100
Agfachrome RSX II 200	200	RSX200
KONICA (www.konica.com)		
Chrome R-100	100	KR100

APPENDIX 9   ADVANCED PHOTO SYSTEM FILMS

(15, 25, or 40 exposure cartridge)

FILM	ISO	FILM CODE
EASTMAN KODAK (www.kodak.com)		
Advantix 100	100	
Advantix 200	200	
Advantix 400	400	
Advantix Black & White + 400	400	

FUJI (www.fujifilm.com)		
Fujicolor Nexia D100	100	
Fujicolor Nexia A200	200	
Fujicolor Nexia H400	400	

AGFA (www.agfa.com)		
Futura 100	100	
Futura 200	200	
Futura 400	400	

KONICA (www.konica.com)		
Centuria 200 APS	200	
Centuria 400 APS	400	

FERRANIA IMAGING TECHNOLOGIES (www.ferraniait.com) (also sold under private label brands)		
Solaris 200	200	
Solaris 400	400	

Glossary

aberration An optical defect in a lens, due to the **A** lens design, that causes blurring or some other type of distortion.

acutance (sharpness) An objective measure of image sharpness. This is tested by placing a knife edge on the film and exposing it to light.

adapter ring A device attached to the front of a lens to allow a filter or another piece of equipment to be fitted to the lens (e.g., may be used to fit a different size filter to the specific filter thread size of the lens).

Advanced Photo System (APS) A photographic system that integrates silver-halide photography and digital information.

American National Standards Institute (ANSI) An organization, formerly called the American Standards Association (ASA), that develops methods of measuring and testing for the purpose of setting standards. For many years ASA was the system used to rate the light sensitivity of photographic materials.

American Standards Association (ASA) See *American National Standards Institute.*

angle of acceptance See *angle of view.*

angle of view The area of a scene that a lens (or

meter) can cover. Varies with the focal length of the lens.

antihalation backing A coating of dye/pigment on the back of film that absorbs any light penetrating through the emulsion, preventing internal flare or reflection.

aperture An opening, usually in or near a lens, that allows light to enter the camera and strike the film.

aperture priority An automatic (A) feature that allows the photographer to choose the aperture (f-stop), with the camera automatically selecting the shutter speed.

APS See *Advanced Photo System.*

array A series of sensors, all of which are the same size and type, referenced by a single identifier,as in a matrix.

autofocus (AF) On certain camera systems, the ability of the camera to automatically focus the lens.

auto-load A feature used on certain cameras to simplify film loading. The photographer places the film cassette in the film chamber, stretches the leader to a specific mark near the take-up spool, and closes the camera back. The camera automatically engages and winds the film onto the take-up reel. This feature is helpful for those who have difficulty manually threading film onto the take-up reel.

automatic exposure (AE) An automatic metering system that allows the camera to determine and set the aperture, shutter speed, or both. See *aperture priority (AP), shutter speed priority (SP),* and *program mode (P).*

automatic mode (A) See *Automatic Exposure.*

auto-rewind On certain motorized cameras, the ability to engage a switch to automatically rewind film from the take-up spool back into the cassette.

auto-thyristor A metering device used to cut off

the flash when the proper exposure has been re-corded on the film. Usually found inside the flash unit.

auto-wind   On certain motorized cameras, the ability of the camera to automatically advance film to the next frame.

available light   See *existing light.*

averaging meter   Reflected-light meter that is sensitive to the entire range covered by the lens.

back light   Illumination that comes from behind the subject (shadow is cast forward).

between-the-lens shutter   See *leaf shutter.*

bounce flash   Diffused illumination caused by directing head of flash unit away from the sub-ject. The flash may be "bounced" off a card, ceil-ing, or wall, producing a softer light.

bracketing   Intentional over and under expo-sure on either side of a designated exposure.

bulb (B)   A shutter speed setting that allows the shutter to remain open for as long as the shutter release is depressed. Used for long exposures.

(C)   The term "Classic" in APS photography. As a print it has an aspect ratio of 2:3, similar to 35 mm format.

cable release   A flexible cable that usually screws into the shutter release button to allow the shutter to be released without touching the camera. Used to reduce camera movement on long exposures.

camera back   1. The door that swings open on a camera to allow the film to be loaded; usually holds the pressure plate. 2. The part of an inter-changeable camera system that holds the film.

camera obscura   "Dark room" (Latin). Initially a darkened room with a small hole in one wall which formed on the opposite wall a scene from outside the room. The precursor of the camera as we know it.

B

C

cassette A light-proof container that holds roll film wound on a spool.

CCD See *charge-coupled device.*

CC filters See *color compensating filters.*

center-weighted A metering system that "biases" the exposure towards what is in the center of the viewfinder.

charge-coupled device A semiconductor device arrayed so that the electric charge at the output of one provides the input stimulus to the next.

chromes See *positive film.*

circles of confusion The relative size of the points of light reflecting from a subject and projected by a lens. The degree of "sharpness" is relative to the size of the discs, or circles, that these points of light create.

close-up A term used for a tightly cropped or composed composition; a photograph in which the subject appears closer than expected.

color balance The accuracy of color film or color prints in matching the colors of the original scene.

color compensating (CC) filters These filters are generally used by professionals for very precise and subtle changes in color. Filters exist in red, green, blue, cyan, magenta, and yellow.

color saturation Subjective reference to the density of a color.

connection terminal The location on a digital camera that allows a cable to be connected to a peripheral piece of equipment.

contact point A metallic surface that allows the flow of electricity between batteries and pieces of equipment.

contrast The range that exists between extremes. Often refers to the range between the light and dark parts of a scene.

conversion filters Filters used to adjust the

color temperature of a light source to match the color temperature of the film, in order to produce a correct color balance.

copy-stand A baseboard with a column and a camera mount, which allows a camera to be moved up or down the column. Usually used when photographing flat work. The baseboard might have extension arms with lights attached, for lighting the subject on the baseboard.

daylight Natural illumination. A color temperature for photographic color materials of 5500K.

D

"dedicated" Used to describe a piece of equipment made for a specific camera model (e.g., dedicated flash).

"dedicated" flash A flash unit made for a specific camera that provides automatic exposure as well as other functions, depending on the camera system.

depth-of-field The range in front of and behind the sharpest point of focus that is acceptably sharp; the range between the nearest and farthest subject distance that is in acceptably sharp focus.

"depth-of-field" mode A setting on some "automatic" cameras that allows the camera to automatically select the aperture needed to record the desired "depth of field."

depth-of-field preview A button or switch that will close the lens aperture to the selected f-stop so that the photographer can preview the "depth of field" before taking a photograph.

depth-of-field scale On some lenses, a scale with f-stop markings located between the f-stop scale and the focusing ring scale. These markings are symmetrically placed on either side of the focusing index mark.

diaphragm A device of overlapping leaves for controlling the size of the aperture, which regulates the amount of light traveling through the lens.

digital camera A camera that records the image as pixel information via a CCD sensor.

digital film back A special attachment for medium and large format cameras that replaces the standard film holder. Used for transforming a traditional film camera to a digital camera system.

digital zoom Magnification of image is either increased or decreased from the original digital input. Information is either added or eliminated in order to fill the entire "frame."

DIN (Deutsche Industrie Normen) A European standard for rating film sensitivity, which is based on a logarithmic progression.

DX code An electrical patch code system on the film cassette that allows certain cameras to automatically set the camera to the correct ISO. The DX code also includes a machine-readable bar code on the cassette and a punched hole raster pattern in the film leader, which processing labs can use for identification of the film.

DX override The ability of some DX cameras to override the automatic DX code setting, changing the ISO.

E **18% reflectance** The mid-point of the photographic gray scale; Zone V. The percentage of light reflectance to which exposure meters are calibrated.

emulsion The light-sensitive coating on a film or paper base, made of gelatin, silver halide salts, and other chemicals.

equivalent exposure An f-stop and shutter speed combination that is equivalent to another combination, neither increasing nor decreasing the amount of light necessary for a proper exposure.

existing light The light that exists without supplemental lighting such as strobe flash; available light.

exposure The amount of light reaching the light-sensitive material, due to the aperture opening (illuminance admitted) and the shutter speed (time). The act of letting light strike the emulsion.

exposure compensation dial An override of the automatic exposure, usually one or two stops over or under the designated "normal" exposure.

exposure index (EI) A numerical numbering system used in measuring the light sensitivity of photographic materials. The lower the EI number, the less sensitive the material is to light. Other systems include ASA, DIN, and ISO.

exposure memory lock A feature that allows some automatic cameras to take a meter reading off one part of the scene and use it to determine the overall exposure.

exposure meter See *light meter.*

film A transparent, thin, flexible material, which is   **F** coated on one side with a light sensitive emulsion. See *emulsion.*

film advance lever A mechanism used to wind fresh film behind the shutter. On most cameras, this lever also advances the film counter number and sets the shutter.

film chamber Area where the film cassette resides in the camera body.

film counter Mechanism that designates the number of "shots" exposed on the roll of film.

film leader In 35 mm photography, the half-width of film at the beginning of a roll, which is used for loading the film. Also called "leader."

film scanner A device for digitizing silver-based film.

film speed The sensitivity of film to light, designated by an ISO number.

filter factor A multiplication factor used to determine correct exposure when a filter is mounted on a lens.

filter A glass, gelatin, plastic, or acetate device placed in front of a lens in order to alter the "regular" exposure, usually by selectively absorbing some of the wavelengths of light travelling through it. See also color compensating filters, conversion filters, gelatin filter, haze filters, neutral density filter, polarizing filter, skylight filter, ultraviolet filter.

flash The artificial illumination caused by an electronic flash unit (strobe).

flash-fill The use of a flash unit in outdoor photography to supplement available daylight.

f-number See *f-stop.*

focal length The distance from the optical center (rear nodal point) of the lens to the plane of sharp focus, when the lens is focused at infinity.

focal plane shutter A shutter built into the camera body as close as possible to the film plane.

focus To make sharp. When film is at the proper focal point for the distance of the object, the image is in focus.

focus-lock A device on auto-focus camera systems that can lock a specific object into focus, to allow a different framing without losing the desired focus target.

focus scale The scale marked with feet/meters on the focusing ring.

focusing index mark A symbol or line on the lens barrel (the center mark, if a depth-of-field scale is present), that points to the distance of the focused object on the focus scale.

focusing ring The part of a lens that moves the lens closer to or farther away from the film plane, in order to make the subject sharp. May have a focus scale on it.

focusing screen The ground-glass mechanism in the camera viewing system that aids in focusing an image. In certain cameras the focusing screen is interchangeable.

format The dimensions of the film image, determined by the template and film size.

front light Light that casts a shadow behind the subject.

f-stop The number that results from dividing the focal length of a lens by the effective diameter of its aperture. Also called the f-number.

gelatin filter A thin dyed and lacquered piece of gelatin used as a filter. **G**

gels Slang for gelatin filters.

grain Refers to the size of the clumping of developed silver in a negative.

Guide Number (G.N.) A number rating system for flash units that is used to calculate the f-stop based on film speed and flash-to-subject distance.

(H) The term "High Definition" in APS photography, the full-frame negative. As a print it has an aspect ratio of 9:16, the universal standard for HDTV. **H**

"haze" filters A category of clear filters that include "UV" and "skylight" filters used to reduce haze and ultraviolet light (excess blue in color film).

hot shoe A bracket on the top of a camera with an electrical contact point. When a flash unit is mounted on the shoe, the contact point will trigger the flash in synchrony with the shutter.

hyperfocal distance The distance to the nearest point of focus when the lens is focused at infinity.

hyperfocal focusing Focusing on the hyperfocal distance, thus creating the maximum possible depth of field.

illuminance The intensity of light falling upon the subject, measured with an incident-light meter. **I**

image compression The reduction in the size of a digital file in order to increase storage capacity.

image mask   In APS photography, the crop marks in the viewfinder and on each frame of the index print, used to choose the format.

image size The magnification of the subject created by a lens. Varies with the focal length and subject distance.

incident meter   A hand-held exposure (light) meter, which measures the amount of light falling upon the subject.

index print   A print with thumbnail-sized photographs of each frame from a roll of APS film. This index print serves as a reference for the photographer in making reprints and enlargements. All three aspect ratios are marked on each frame.

Information Exchange (IX) In APS photography, the ability to exchange information between photographer, camera, film, and photofinishing equipment, made possible by the magnetic coating on the surface of the film.

International Organization for Standardization (ISO)   The organization that devised the most commonly accepted exposure index (EI) standards. A combination of the ASA and DIN systems.

iris diaphragm   See *diaphragm.*

iris shutter   See *leaf shutter.*

ISO   See *International Organization for Standardization.*

IX   See *Information Exchange.*

L   **latitude** The amount of over and under exposure a film allows with acceptable results.

LCD (liquid crystal display) An electronic display window that can form numbers, symbols, etc. Used in many cameras and meters with digital readout.

leader   See *film leader.*

leaf shutter   A shutter with overlapping blades

that are mechanically or electronically controlled to admit light through the lens for a specific amount of time.

LED (light emitting diode) An electronic flashing light designating information; usually found within the viewfinder.

lens Optical glass (or other transparent material) that forces rays of light to diverge or converge to form an image.

lens barrel The tube of the lens housing the various lens elements.

lens element A single piece of glass that is a lens or part of a compound lens. A compound lens is made of many lens elements.

light The visible part of the electromagnetic spectrum (400 – 700nm).

light balancing Matching the color temperature of the light source to the color temperature of the film. See *conversion filters.*

light emitting diode See *LED*.

light meter A device, either built into the camera or separate, that measures the intensity of light present and indicates an f-stop and shutter speed combination for proper exposure, based on the film speed.

liquid crystal display See *LCD*.

luminance The intensity of light reflecting off or emanating from a subject. Measured with a reflected-light meter.

LZW (Lempel-Ziv-Welch) A "lossless" digital image compression system. There is no loss of digital information.

"M" Symbol used for "manual." Also the symbol used on some shutters to designate the setting for M-class flashbulb synchronization (flashbulbs that are rarely in use today).   **M**

macro lens Specially designed lens that extends its normal focusing to include close-up photography.

Lens designed for optimum image quality, correcting common problems in close-up photography.

manual (M) override On automatic exposure cameras, the ability to override the automatic settings and set exposure functions manually. On autofocus cameras, the ability to override the automatic setting to manually focus.

manual switch See *depth-of-field preview*.

matrix meter A meter design that reads light from a myriad of sensors and analyzes the information through a microprocessor.

maximum effective aperture The largest or maximum possible f-stop opening of a lens. The speed of a lens.

megapixel A term to describe digital cameras that can record at least one million pixels.

memory Refers to the size of the image storage capacity in a digital camera or disk.

N **neutral density (ND) filter** A filter that evenly absorbs the wavelengths of light, without affecting color balance.

normal lens A lens with a focal length that is close to the diagonal of the film plane; a lens that does not magnify or reduce the objects in a scene. Most closely reproduces the scene as viewed by the human eye.

O **optical zoom** In a digital camera with an optical zoom, the optics of the lens creates the change in the focal length magnification.

P **(P)** The term "Panorama" in APS photography. As a print it has an aspect ratio of 1:3.

panning A technique in which the camera is moved along with a moving subject during exposure. The result is that the moving subject remains relatively sharp and the background becomes blurred in the photograph.

parallax error In rangefinder cameras, the angle-of-view difference between the viewfinder image and the image the lens records. Significant in close-up and copy-stand photography.

pentaprism The part of the viewing system of single lens reflex cameras that receives the light from the mirror and directs it to the eyepiece.

perspective The relative size of objects in relation to their distance from the camera. Altered by camera to subject distance only.

pixel Short term for picture element. A single point in a graphic image.

polarizing filter A filter that polarizes light in order to reduce reflections and glare from non-metallic surfaces.

port See *connection terminal.*

portrait lens A slight telephoto lens used for head and shoulder portraits.

"positive" film A transparent film that matches the tones or colors of the original scene. Also called color transparency, reversal film, slide film, and "chromes."

pressure plate A spring-mounted plate, located on the camera back, that holds the film flat against the template and parallel to the lens plane.

prism See *pentaprism.*

program mode (P) An automatic metering function that sets the camera to an f-stop and shutter speed chosen from a pre-determined set of combinations.

rangefinder An optical device in a viewfinder that focuses the lens by determining the camera-to-subject distance.   **R**

rear nodal point In a compound lens, the position from which the focal length is determined; similar to the optical center of a simple lens.

reciprocity correction A specific exposure increase that corrects for reciprocity failure.

reciprocity failure   Failure of a film to follow the reciprocity law. This occurs in very long or very short exposures.

reciprocity law   When Exposure (E) = Intensity (I) x Time (T). This reciprocal relationship allows for equivalent exposure settings.

red eye   A red spot in the center of the eyes of people or animals. This occurs in photographs when the light rays from the flash unit reflect off the blood vessels of the retina.

reflected-light meter   A light meter that reads the light reflecting off or emitted from the objects in the field.

relative motion The apparent speed of a moving object, based on actual speed, distance, and direction.

resolving power (resolution)   The ability of a film or digitized image to reproduce fine detail.

revealing light   The broad, diffused light that exists on an overcast day, or the light cast by fluorescent lights. Shadows are evenly dispersed.

reversal film   See *positive film.*

rewind crank   Mechanical gear used to rewind film from the take-up spool back into the film cassette.

rewind release button or switch   Disengages the sprocket wheel gear, allowing the film to rewind.

rule of f/16   A method of estimating an exposure at f/16, if no light meter is available.

S   **self-timer**   A mechanism (usually built into the camera) that delays the operation of the shutter for a few seconds after the shutter release button has been "tripped."

shoe   A bracket that is used to attach a flash unit to a camera, bracket grip, or other device. See *hot shoe.*

shutter A mechanism that opens and closes at a controlled interval of time, allowing light to expose the film in the camera.

shutter release button The "trigger" or lever that, when depressed, allows the shutter mechanism to operate.

shutter speed The designated length of time for an exposure, indicated by the marking selected on the shutter speed dial.

shutter-speed priority (SP) An automatic camera operating mode. When using SP, the photographer sets a shutter speed and the camera automatically selects the appropriate f-number for correct exposure.

side light A directional light that casts a shadow to one side of the subject.

silver halide A compound of silver and halogen salt, which is the light-sensitive substance in photographic emulsions.

single-lens reflex (SLR) A type of camera that allows the photographer to view and compose through the lens by means of a mirror-prism system.

skylight filter A filter that reduces excess blue in color films. Often used as a lens protector. See *haze filters.*

slide film See *positive film.*

software Computer instructions or data.

spectral sensitivity The degree or range of sensitivity of film to visible light on the electromagnetic spectrum.

"speed" (of a lens) See *maximum effective aperture.*

spot meter A light-meter that uses a very narrow angle of light for its sensor.

sprocket wheel Engages the film's sprocket holes in order to pull fresh film forward.

stop A change of either half or double the preceding exposure, in either the aperture or the shutter speed.

sync cord A special cord (PC cord) that makes

the electrical link between a flash unit and a camera body, by connecting the flash unit to the sync terminal.

sync speed   The fastest shutter speed on a focal plane shutter camera that allows for flash synchronization.

synchronization (sync) terminal   The receptacle on the camera body for the PC terminal of the sync cord.

T   **take-up spool**   The mechanism on which the "exposed" film is wound.

"taking" lens   The lens that records the image on the film.

teleconverter   An attachment that fits between the lens and the camera body, effectively increasing the focal length of the lens.

telephoto lens   A general term for a lens whose focal length is longer than the diagonal of the film. A lens that is longer than a "normal" lens.

template   The rectangular window in the camera body near the focal plane, which creates the format size of the film.

through-the-lens (TTL)   The measuring of light after it passes through the lens.

through-the-lens (TTL) flash metering   A sensor at the film plane in dedicated flash systems, which shuts the flash off when it senses the proper quantity of light.

thyristor circuit   The electronic switch that automatically shuts down the flash when proper exposure has been achieved, and stores the saved power in the capacitor.

TIFF (Tagged Image File Format)   A "lossy" digital image compression system. Some digital information is sacrificed in the process.

time exposure   Generally refers to any long exposure that needs to be timed manually. Time exposures are usually longer than one second.

transparency film See *positive film.*

tripod A three-legged adjustable stand for support of a camera, usually with a tilting and swivelling platform (head) on which the camera is secured.

tripod mount The threaded receptacle on the bottom of a camera, which is used to secure the tripod screw.

tungsten light Light produced by photographic incandescent lamps with a 3200K or 3400K color temperature. Also, a general term for standard filament lightbulbs.

ultraviolet (UV) filter A filter that reduces the amount of ultraviolet light striking the film.

U

viewfinder The complex viewing system that allows for focusing and composing the photograph.

V

wide angle lens A lens whose focal length is shorter than the diagonal of the film plane. A lens that is shorter than a "normal" lens.

W

Wratten filter numbers The most widely used number system for describing and identifying filters.

x-rays A part of the electromagnetic spectrum that can have a detrimental effect on film emulsion.

X

zone In the zone system, the tone or luminance of a subject when rendered in the print. Each zone from 0 – IX is a one-stop difference from its adjacent zone.

Z

zone focus A method of determining the specific depth-of-field by selecting the near and far boundaries of focus.

zone system A method of exposure and development, and a way to describe the tonal translation of a subject's luminance to its corresponding print density.

Zone V In the *zone system*, the mid-gray value of 18% reflectance.

zoom lens A lens that has a continuous selection of focal lengths within its designated range.

Index